CONSTITUTIONAL CRACK-UP
CANADA AND THE COMING SHOWDOWN WITH QUEBEC

WILLIAM D. GAIRDNER

For Kenneth McDonald,
author, teacher, and gentleman,
who saw it all coming long ago

Published in 1994 by
Stoddart Publishing Co. Limited
34 Lesmill Road
Toronto, Canada
M3B 2T6
(416) 445-3333

A brief version of this essay appeared in the revised edition of the
author's *The Trouble With Canada*.

William D. Gairdner publishes *Speaking Out*, a newsletter on political,
economic, and social issues. For more information, write to "Newsletter,"
255 Yorkland Boulevard, Suite 220, Willowdale, Ontario, Canada M2J 1S3.

Cover Design: Brant Cowie/Artplus Limited
Printed and bound in Canada

Contents

France is a country that lives by the statute book.
For us, the law, once written, is sacred. It can be
altered only in the most solemn circumstances.
Britain, on the other hand, is famous for its
pragmatism. Its law is that of custom and usage,
constantly adapting to new conditions.

Maurice Couve de Murville, French Statesman

The notion that personal liberty is a special
privilege insured . . . by some power above the ordinary
laws of the land . . . is an idea utterly alien
to English modes of thought.

A. V. Dicey, *The Law of the Constitution*

In general I commit myself to the position that we are living in a
world that in certain important respects has gone wrong on first
principles; which [is] only another way of saying that we are living
in a world that has been betrayed by its leaders.

Irving Babbitt, *Democracy and Leadership*, 1924

There never was a democracy
that did not commit suicide.

John Adams, Second President of the United States

Introduction

What in the world is happening to Canada? How can a radical separatist from Quebec serve as Her Majesty's loyal Opposition? How could a country of sensible people deteriorate from a condition of rock-solid financial stability into a country with the second largest per-capita debt in the developed world in the mere space of twenty-five years? Why is Canada, one of the world's noblest experiments in democracy, coming apart at the seams?

The answer to our future lies in a deeper understanding of our recent past. For Canada is a country that has been utterly changed in very recent times without the moral sanction of its people; ripped, as it were, from its founding principles and values, and thrown into crisis by self-serving politicians and ideologues. This looming crisis will exact — is already exacting — a grave financial, moral, and political price. Meanwhile, the people as a whole seem to be sleepwalking into a dark night.

So this is a wake-up call. For the solution to Canada's crisis will not likely come from politicians. They're the ones who dug the hole we are in. Any solution must come from the people; we need a much broader awareness of how the fundamental characteristics of Canada have been altered by our leaders, and, more importantly, of what may be done to reconstitute the nation on its founding principles.

Readers are first invited to explore in some depth the most basic and fundamental questions concerning their Constitution, and to understand how their personal rights and freedoms have been changed and diminished since the 1960s.

Then they are asked to consider some of the fundamentals of a good and true constitution, in contrast to which our Charter of Rights and Freedoms suffers greatly.

Next, and perhaps most importantly, they will see why it is that documents such as our Charter, while ostensibly designed to preserve society, in fact preserve government instead, while attacking society at its very heart; why a written charter and a natural civil society are antithetical.

Finally, there is an overview of the difficulties we will soon experience over "the problem of Quebec," which is, in fact, not just Quebec's problem, but a national problem intimately linked to, and flowing directly from, our constitutional crack-up.

I
-

WHAT *IS* A CONSTITUTION, ANYWAY

Is It for the People, or for the State?

We are often told that the only two certainties in life are death and taxes. But there is a third. It's not quite as obvious, perhaps, but just as certain.

The daily conduct, freedoms, and restraints of all people everywhere are indelibly affected and bounded by their nation's constitution. And yet this pervasive, controlling force is largely invisible. It is an abstract presence that so thoroughly permeates and orders the concrete relations of everyday life we are largely unaware of it, in the same way that we live within our own bodies without being much aware of our breathing.

Unless we wish to live as hermits, or wander the world as rootless adventurers, we cannot escape this control. We can alter it by moving to a different place. But then we must live under the constitution of some other people, or nation. For wherever two or more are gathered together, a society, and then right on its heels, a constitution — a set of conventions, rules, and laws of mutual conduct — must spring up.

Neither can we escape this certainty by saying "Let's get rid of it!" or, "Who needs a constitution, anyway?" For even if never written down, the slowly evolving moral and legal principles, customs, and conventions of a nation, when considered as a whole, are its "constitution," within the confines of which, for better or worse, all citizens are bound.

For it is the constitution that ultimately dictates the freedom with which we may condemn the government in our local newspaper without fear of a midnight visit from police; but it is also the constitution that gives those police the right to lock us up, confiscate our private files, garnishee our wages, and appropriate our homes if, for example, we refuse to give the State half of our hard-earned income in taxes each year.

Throughout history, the powers that be may bind the people unbearably through pervasive and minute regulation, taxation, or overtly repressive measures sanctioned by some constitution or other. And from this, the people may seek to escape. The history of human migration, often in the face of grave danger and privation, has etched in our consciousness an image peculiar to our time, one that attests to the stirring reality of these escapes. It is by now an archetype. On the one hand, we see a zealous official holding up a stern legal constitution enforcing some cruel ideological program; on the other, we see shivering, hungry, and frightened citizens clinging to battered boats in frigid seas, or trampling over alien mountains, their only nourishment the hope of freedom at last. At bottom, much of the sweeping and romantic span of North American settlement for half a millennium was and still is motivated by an urgency to escape some cloying, oppressive, and yes, very legal constitution back home. These people are fleeing an almighty piece of paper.

Because such major oppressions begin in minor ways, the question all citizens, even those of the freer nations such as our own, need to consider very deeply is whether or not they need a written constitution, and if they do, what kind it should be. For it is the obvious purpose of all *written* constitutions to arrest the slowly evolving changes of the unwritten constitutional framework, in order to petrify what some consider to be current political perfections and — not incidentally — to make the exercise of power permanent and unchanging. Some? Well then, who? And for what purpose? The realities of daily life, of politics, values, freedoms, and rights, change constantly throughout history, sometimes with each change of government, and this is disturbing. Hence the desire to nail everything down once and for all and "put it in writing."

But we must be wary, for the pen truly is mightier than the sword. If, as Aristotle warned us, what is put in writing — the written constitution — fails to protect and promote the basic formative values of the people, or has only weak support from the governed, or fails to allow for adaptation to changing circumstances, or, as I shall argue, if it becomes an instrument used by elites to engineer the outcomes of civil society against the deeper wishes of the people, it will eventually tear the country apart more surely than any invading army could ever do.

WHAT IS CANADA'S WRITTEN CONSTITUTION?

Canada's founding constitutional document is called the British North America Act, 1867 (BNA Act). It was created by our founding fathers to join into one nation what were then the provinces of Nova Scotia, New Brunswick, and "Canada." (Under the act, the province of Canada was subdivided into Lower Canada and Upper Canada, which became Ontario and Quebec, respectively.) All four provinces agreed to become united under the name of the "Dominion of Canada," each with its own legislature and powers, and all under a single executive government, now known as the federal government.

Because the founders were extremely wary of big government tyranny, the act clearly and specifically divided governmental powers and duties between the federal government and the provinces in order to block any monopoly of power that could be suffered upon a minority of the people by raw majority rule. There were various provincial domains the federal government could not enter. For example, health care, education, and welfare were to be strictly provincial matters. Democracy, after all, had sanctioned despotism in Europe, and slavery in the United States. So the hobble of strictly divided powers and spending authority was felt to be the antidote to big government.

The BNA Act was primarily a sober, uninspiring organizational and administrative document. It said almost nothing about "human rights," or duties, on the firm grounds that these two things cannot be separated, and that within the framework of a good government designed to protect freedom, family, free enterprise, and faith, they will spring naturally from personal and community conduct.

But the idealist mentality is a restless one, and by the mid-twentieth century, a variety of Canadian leaders pushed for a "Bill of Rights" (subsequently echoed by each province) and for "entrenchment" of such rights in our Constitution. Somehow, the more democratic societies lose their grip on the notion of personal moral control, the more so-called rights have to be spelled out, publicly proclaimed, protected, and policed. It was a bad sign. A move away from conduct, towards contract.

The idealist vision was achieved under Prime Minister Pierre Elliott Trudeau with the Constitution Act, 1982, otherwise known as the Charter of Rights and Freedoms. This was a document that formalized and entrenched not only a set of rights, but indeed an entire State enterprise for the reshaping of Canada, and the control of a resurgent Quebec. I will argue that it served a variety of political purposes, mostly unrelated to our true Constitution.

DOES LEGITIMACY DERIVE FROM
THE GOVERNED . . .

As civilized nations grope their way towards a satisfactory style of operation, one that combines sufficient protections for the freedom of individuals with sufficient leeway for the State to perform its role, the most fundamental question must always be: What is the proper role of the State?

Until that question is answered and echoed in the hearts and minds of the people, we cannot say to what degree basic individual rights and freedoms ought to be limited. In the ideal democratic State, the concept of personal rights, freedoms, and duties would be all-important. The State would refuse to engage in the sort of social engineering of which modern liberals have grown so fond, and would allow itself very little room to manoeuvre beyond the setting of rules of just conduct, equal for all. No exceptions.

In this view, the only moral justification for the existence of the State is to serve and defend the civil society of the people, to uphold the laws, and to keep the peace, and if the people don't like the way a particular government does this, they can change it. That is what we are taught in school. The classical principle, fiercely defended throughout history, is that the powers required by government at the top are derived from the consent of the governed at the bottom, and that without such consent these powers can have no possible legitimacy. This is the vision of democracy, from ancient Athens, to the modern town hall meeting, that stirs the souls of freedom lovers everywhere, and always has.* But it is a much-dreamt dream that is seldom lived. As the gap ever widens between the will of the people and the actions of modern governments, citizens all over the democratic world are increasingly questioning the basic legitimacy of the State.

. . . OR FROM THE GOVERNORS?

In collectivist regimes, however (and only an understanding of the extremes enables us to see the shadings), this thinking is completely reversed. Legitimacy flows from the top downwards. As a matter of national philosophy and law, the individual is considered utterly subordinate to the State, and any collection of self-interested individuals is considered a mere — at worst a mean — mob. In fact, to a pure collectivist, the very idea of a single individual having any rights whatsoever against the State is outrageous, an offence against the truth, even treasonous. So whether hard socialist, communist, or fascist, all collectivists (this includes the soft modern term "centralist") in varying degrees venerate the State as the only force capable of unifying the scattered masses, of

---

* *Many of us have at one time or another stood up in some gathering and declared of some decision, "That's not democratic!" We get very emotional at the democratic spectacle. So it comes as a great surprise to learn that neither the founders of Canada nor the United States were seeking to form a "democracy." On the contrary, a pure democracy was what they feared. To most of them a pure democracy, in which the will of the people reigned, was a licence for mob rule, for history has shown and they believed deeply that in such a democracy, the eternal and transcendent rights of individuals — of the forty-nine percent — would be quickly trampled. So while both nations wanted to include certain democratic*

focusing the lives of millions of individuals whose disparate wills, they fear, would otherwise fragment the State.

Many Canadian politicians, from Confederation in 1867 to the present, have gone public with the view that the only thing that constitutes our special value system and holds the nation together — other than the railroad — are the collective programs and institutions of the welfare State. Prime Minister Trudeau, the grand architect of Canadian socialism who has always described himself as a freedom fighter (despite the obvious fact that socialism and freedom cannot sleep in the same bed), has argued repeatedly throughout his career for the unifying values of statism, within a federal context. In 1968 he declared in his book *Federalism and the French Canadians* that "federalism must be welcomed as a valuable tool which permits dynamic parties *to plant socialist governments in certain provinces, from which the seeds of radicalism can spread*," and that "a socialist must be a centralizer."[1] Four years earlier, in *Cité Libre,* he wrote that "the very purpose of a collective system is better to ensure personal freedom." In other words, he constantly promoted the modern liberal idea that in order to be more free, you need more government.

---

rights, the likelihood of mob rule was to be severely checked by unelected upper houses, by wide prime ministerial, and cabinet (or presidential) powers, by various ad hoc instruments and vetoes, and so on — all very undemocratic methods, indeed. The search was for a democratic process, limited and bound by humane institutional checks and balances. It was James Madison, a central force in the formation of the American Constitution, who warned the world, "Hold fast to programs, both rational and moral, that have, as their central goal, a constant diffusion of power, for in no man or government does great power safely reside."

ROUSSEAU: THE FRENCH CONNECTION

This statement sounds absurdly contradictory to anyone raised under an English-style governance, because the English idea is that personal freedom is a natural right, and the only legitimate function of government is to create an environment wherein freedom may be expressed, under laws equal for all. We agree to surrender some freedom for those necessary laws, even though we know our freedom is in natural conflict with them. But those raised in the contrary, French-style school of government promote the notion that more of the right kind of government reduces or even removes human conflict, thus freeing people to be good, orderly citizens. In other words, subordination to the rule of the governors makes you free. In this, Trudeau was and remains a slavish and uncritical disciple of his political mentor, the Swiss-French philosopher Jean-Jacques Rousseau (1712-1778), whose ideas changed the face of Europe and are still present in modern liberal thought. Maximilien Robespierre (1758-1794), architect of the bloody French Terror, was a direct disciple of Rousseau who clutched his teacher's books to his breast like sacred sripture as he sent hundreds of thousands of French citizens to the guillotine in the name of the public good. Eventually, these same ideas sent Robespierre himself to the guillotine. What exactly did Rousseau say, such that a politician like Trudeau would quote him as his authority for the growth of big government in Canada, two centuries later?

THE GENERAL WILL

Rousseau is considered by many scholars to be the father of the Romantic movement (to be explained below). He was and remains a hero to all leftists, who see him as the prophet of democracy, while conservatives see him as the progenitor of modern totalitarian thought, for reasons to be mentioned shortly. At any rate, his books, especially *The Social Contract*, are taught to aspiring democrats in political science departments all over the world (yes, Premier Bob Rae of Ontario, with his own pedestrian "social contract," is another fan of this thinking).

As Stephen Clarkson and Christina McCall wrote in their bestseller *Trudeau and Our Times*, it was at the London School of Economics in 1948 that Trudeau "made a surprisingly sharp turn to the left," "attached himself" to "his mentor" Harold Laski, who was by then Great Britain's "most powerful spokesman for socialism," and "positioned himself for the first time decidedly on the political left."[2]

At LSE, Trudeau became sufficiently infatuated with Rousseau to rely on him in a casual but dangerous way as one of his two lifelong political authorities. The other, paradoxically, was John Locke, defender of the English notion of politics: free individuals forming a civil society with the State serving only as referee, thus vesting maximum power in the people. The source of the famous "contradictory" political personality of Pierre Trudeau — this son of a Scottish mother and French-Canadian father — can be found in his affections for the contradictory and irreconcilable philosophies of Locke and Rousseau.

Clarkson and McCall barely mention Rousseau in their book, thus missing the key to Trudeau's political thinking.[3] But they do say that

> from Rousseau [Trudeau] retained the democratic view that, in the ideal state, citizens enter a social contract in which they consent to obey laws that are the product of their own general will. In the actual political systems he studied, constitutions were simply the means necessary to achieve the desired end.[4]

This is a crucial observation: that Trudeau (and all social engineers like him) see a constitution not as an end in itself, a refereeing device for allowing people to live within their own mould under the law, but *as a means to the achievement of some ideal State*, an instrument for forcing society into a predetermined social and political mould.*

Let us now consider why Rousseau's thinking excited Trudeau so much.

Rousseau was a Romantic thinker who argued that men are born free, but are everywhere in chains, by which he meant the chains of authority created by church, State, family, morality,

---

* *Although specific reference to Rousseau is sparse in Trudeau's* Federalism and the French Canadians, *we can easily see through him to Rousseau, especially in the essay "Federalism, Nationalism, and Reason," based, as it is, on Rousseau's notion of the General Will (la volonté générale). Trudeau repeats everywhere in his own way that "the foundation of the nation is will" (p. 187); "for there is no power without will" (p. 187). "Self-determination was based on will," he writes (p. 184); an international order would be founded on "the free will of the people," "willing their way toward statehood." On page 195 he repeats the phrase "will of the people" four times in one paragraph. At the end of his career, in his*

and so on. If all men are born good, but in practice do bad things, it is not their own fault, but the fault of their environment, which keeps them ignorant or enslaved to false ideas. Because all people are born naturally good, then they will be moral if allowed to express themselves. Therefore, the way to have a good society is to shake off all authority, let the goodness thrive unimpeded, allowing the people to express this goodness in the General Will. This General Will is supposed to be a mystical whole comprised of all the competent individual wills in the nation, a sum greater than its parts. Both Rousseau and Trudeau have described it as a "mysterious essence," or "process." Because of this notion, Rousseau is rightly considered, as Felix Morley put it, "the father of untrammelled political democracy."[5]

But also because of it he is rightly considered a scoundrel, because the notion of a "national will," to be shaped and guided by the leaders, a mysterious, or mystical General Will that vests all power in "the people" lies at the heart of all collectivist political philosophy. It is a notion utterly opposed to the English-style idea of faith in the individual, which until recently lay at the basis of British, Canadian, and American government. Under the English-

book *Pierre Trudeau Speaks Out on Meech Lake (1990)*, he seems obsessed with Rousseau's notion of the General Will. He says that sixty years of Canadian federalism from 1927 forward strove "to create a national will," or, "'une volonté générale,' as Rousseau had called it" (p. 45); this Canadian will would be a "body of beliefs" — beliefs in fact designed by Trudeau and his colleagues, and later entrenched in his Charter in 1982. And again, he complained, "with Meech Lake there is no national will left" (p. 66). And again he mentions "the idea of a national will" (p. 67); "the existence of a national will" (p. 67, twice); and then, "denying the existence of a national will" (p. 87).

style system, society is freely formed by individuals within a rule of law. There is no General Will possible, unless under a dictator. This is not to say that such a people cannot act in unison when it suits their purposes; the wars of this century have shown that once aroused they can do this very well. It is merely to say that polities based on the English system make a clear distinction between society and State, and assign to the State the role of referee, not star player. This is in stark contrast to most European polities that make a less forceful distinction between these two roles — indeed, rather expect the State to referee as well as play the game, to guide and shape society. Rousseau's ideas explain why.

Rousseau linked his idea of a General Will to his secondary notion of a Social Contract, and thereby unleashed totalitarian dangers to be suffered upon the West by his intellectual children ever since. For if the General Will is to be effective at all, if all men are born equal, and equally good in their physical, mental, and spiritual composition (*liberté, egalité, fraternité*), then their differences are secondary, and the General Will must be made manifest, by force if necessary. It soon becomes the function of the leaders, therefore, to ensure that this is so, and they can only do this by eliminating as many "disparities," "inequities," and "disadvantages" as possible and by subjecting all differing lives and dissenting wills to rigorous governmental controls. Hence the widespread modern effort to equalize all incomes, lifestyles, attitudes, and material outcomes. This must be done, because the General Will, as Rousseau put it, "is always right, and always tends toward the Public Good."

The assumption soon develops that only enemies of the nation could possibly oppose the General Will, and that the majority is always right. Dissenters are soon defined as outlaws, or "enemies of the people" (or in our case "enemies of Canada") who must, depending on the degree of fanaticism, be first silenced (via public and media scorn), then if necessary punished (summoned, sentenced, fined, by unelected tribunals), then jailed or exterminated (when this process really gets out of hand). For a single will soon requires a single unified governmental direction. The grossly interventionist, high-taxation, perversely regulatory welfare State, replete with its hundreds of agencies and employees (one for every 5.5 citizens in Canada), is our genteel version of this.

Morley points out that the fallacy of this statist philosophy is that it is always up to some ruler(s) to interpret the General Will, then impose it on the people as law. Those who refuse to follow the General Will, as Rousseau put it, "will be forced to be free."[6] Of course the lie was given to the whole idea of the General Will at a very early stage of the French Terror, when Robespierre and the Committee of Public Safety he ran voted to behead Louis XVI in the name of the General Will. The vote was an extremely bitter and divisive 387 to 334. There was nothing "general" about this decision — one that changed the course of modern history — and nothing could more clearly demonstrate the way in which Rousseau's clever notion mutates into a claptrap pseudo-mystical excuse for the exercise of raw power by whichever group or individual has been able to seize it (in the name of the people, of course).

The key socialist instruments for "forcing" people to be free under a democratic system are "education" — Trudeau often said "the best way to correct them if they are misinformed is to educate them,"[7] especially through the public schools; fiscal bribery (transfers and subsidies); and constitutional laws that impose some egalitarian vision of utopia. Rousseau said, "You must, therefore, treat citizens as children and control their upbringing and their thoughts, planting the social law in the bottom of their hearts." For him, virtue was the product not of individual moral struggle, but of good government. And surely the single most crushing truth to be drawn from Rousseau's ideas in modern times is that everywhere they have been applied, individual freedom and local government have been denied in the name of centralized power. The great historian Paul Johnson has written that through his influence on Hegel and Marx, Rousseau "set in motion the great stream of ideas which produced the ruthless regimes of the twentieth century . . . since they all practiced the social and cultural engineering of which he was the ideologist."[8] Marx, Stalin, Mussolini, Hitler — all loved Rousseau. Even Trudeau has indicated a begrudging awareness of these twisted realities. In 1991, after citing Rousseau once again to support his argument, he said, "There have been all kinds of interpretations of Rousseau's social contract. Maybe it is the formula for dictatorship."[9] In this halting admission, we can sense Trudeau's fleeting, intuitive fear of his own political theories.

And it is very interesting that both the American and Canadian fathers of federalism, while they may have accepted the basic notion of individual rights *against* the State, *completely rejected* Rousseau's notion of the General Will. Through a rigid division of powers and checks and balances (which we will see have now been largely circumvented in Canada), they strove specifically to prevent the unification of power under any General Will, or big central government.

WHERE THE SOCIALIST DREAM LEADS, IF UNCHECKED

An extreme and extremely clear expression of the collectivist's vision, *à la Rousseau*, which we ought to keep nearby as a warning of our proximity to such dangerous political shoals, can be found in the writings of the Italian dictator Benito Mussolini. I include him here because his thinking represents one polarity of the democratic possibility as it moves from parliamentary socialism (what we have now), to a totalitarian democracy, to real collectivism (which one hopes we will never see here). And I also include him because all modern democracies are in this together. All are thrashing in the same chains, read the same theories, fall victim to the same false logic, the same voting pressures. And they watch and even copy each other. Britain was among the freer nations until the 1960s, when she embraced socialism and sank beneath the waves of debt, surfacing briefly for air under Margaret Thatcher. Canada, to which many Brits fled to escape socialism, then fell for it herself (often pushed there by socialist U.K. immigrants). Lester Pearson and

Trudeau — and much of Europe — have since the 1950s admired the (now sickly) Sweden as "the middle way" between the free market (still roaring today) and the Communist nations (now dead, or terminally ill). So we must strive to understand the polarities to which our own errors may drive us, or dreams lure us. Suffice it to say that throughout history what has driven people to adoration of the State as a unifying force is the chaos in their midst. With sufficient social breakdown, unemployment, crashing financial markets, crime in the streets, and anarchy in the schools, the barometer of fear rises so high that people will accept even a harsh dictator with pleasure and relief.

In 1932, in the midst of such European chaos, Mussolini argued simply and starkly that his brand of collectivism "stresses the importance of the State and accepts the individual only insofar as his interests coincide with those of the State." He said that classical liberalism, because it was based on individual freedom, denied the importance of the State in the name of the individual, whereas his political theory "reasserts the rights of the State as expressing the real essence of the individual." Outside of the State, he declared, "no human or spiritual values can exist."[10] He meant, *will be allowed to exist*. His most famous summary of this attitude is, "Everything within the State, nothing outside the State, nothing against the State."

Hitler's vision of the ant-heap society — a predictable, even an inevitable result whenever the utopian impulse, combined with real power, remains unchecked — outdid even Mussolini's for Orwellian Newspeak. He stamped in steel over the gates of his forced-labour camps the phrase "*Arbeit Macht Frei*," which means "Work will make you free." Freedom is forced labour for the glory of the State in a concentration camp? These are dangerous folks, indeed. The largest single professional group in the Nazi party in its most heady years? Schoolteachers, who enthusiastically promoted the party slogan, "One People, One State, One Leader."[11]

But it is just as easy to find this sort of justification for the all-consuming presence of the State in religious (theocratic) nations for which the State and its holy leaders are deemed an expression of the will of God. To such nations the very idea of democracy, a system that allows popular opposition to the will of government (therefore to the will of God), is considered lunatic, even seditious. Islamic states are an example. And even the Christian states such as Britain, Canada, and the U.S.A. almost until the middle of the twentieth century showed remnants of their belief in the connection between the State and religious belief by barring from public office anyone who failed to swear allegiance to the Christian God. American money still carries as a motto the words "In God We Trust," and the Canadian Charter opens with the assurance that Canada "is founded upon principles that recognize the supremacy of God." But there is an important distinction. The Judeo-Christian states saw God and his law as something above the State, not in it. Job applicants swore on the Bible to say *they* were good, not to say that the State was good. They assumed that because all humans are flawed by nature, just about everything they do, especially when drunk with power, is also flawed, and therefore you need God-fearing officials around with their hands firmly on the tiller of the State.

Secular statists like Marx, Mussolini, and Hitler, however, see the whole idea of a transcendent God, or value system, as inimical to their utopian project, and so they simply deny that there is any divine or moral authority above that of the State. Or they define the entire idea of a transcendent moral system as evil. They don't want the competition. They don't want the people marching to a divine drummer. They don't want anyone saying to their tribunals, "I obey God's law, not man's law." Thus they outlaw the notion, the symbols, and the ceremonies of the transcendent God. But anyone can see what comes next. They are smart enough to know that the human spiritual hunger never disappears. It must somehow be satisfied. So they work very hard to convert utopian ideas of the State itself, or the specialness of their nation or race (usually all of these), into a secular faith, with all the ritualistic trappings and ceremony of mainstream religion. In other words, they bring God down to earth: He really is here, they say, or imply, in the goodness and the godlike works of the State. Conclusion? The State and its ministers will bring about the good life. Heaven on earth. For this shining end, any means are soon justified. Ultimately, when the heads of such dreamers have swelled sufficiently, and after enough blood has been spilled, they try to persuade the people that the divine is in themselves, and more specifically in their leaders, who by now are described with such fawning terms as "Redeemer," "Father," "Duce," "Vozhd´," and so on. Italian, German, Soviet, and Chinese schoolchildren under Mussolini, Hitler, Stalin, and Mao were made to chant poems about the mystical fusion of their leader's soul with their own, and with the the the soul of the State.

CLEANSING FOR THE PUBLIC GOOD

So for Rousseau, the *General Will* was divine. For the Fascists, the *State* was Divine, for there could be nothing higher. For the Communists, the inevitability of *History* and the classless utopian future was divine. For our secular, even rigorously atheistic liberal democracies, what is highest and most sacred is *Equality*. In other words, *human reason working through the State in the service of the egalitarian "Public Good."* Officially, the modern liberal (a traitor to the ideals of his classical liberal parent) argues that there must be only equal individuals beneath the State, and nothing above it. It is the job of the State to eradicate all differences, and promote a kind of uniformitarian conformity to approved, yet simplistic ideals, from which open and public deviation is increasingly discouraged. Next, even private deviations (yes, even personal thoughts and attitudes) are discouraged (and "re-education" prescribed). All uniformitarian regimes — which is what we have in Canada now — move, at first gingerly, then aggressively, against all aspects of civil society that offend the public dogma (in our case, the central public dogma of State-provided equality). Political correctness in our institutions of "higher learning" is simply the most visible symptom of such cleansing behaviour, the boil festering on the body politic.

I have dwelt on this matter simply to warn that the most dangerous form of cleansing ritual is the one done in the name of democracy. Totalitarian nations impose their cleansing regimes from the top, against a shattered and grieving people below, who have never had any illusions about their voting importance. Many of them risked their lives coming to countries like Canada. For them, the enemy is easy to identify. He is the internal police: the sallow-eyed man on the far corner posted to watch your every move. But such rituals under a democratic system are far more dangerous because they rely on the pleasing and powerful marketing muscle of a materialistic, high-tech society to persuade or shame the people into correctness. There is no spy smoking under a lampost at the corner: he is in your living room cajoling you from your own television set. He is on the committee disqualifying your research grant; on the legal reform council altering the laws to reach more deeply into your private life. The marketing objective here is the recruitment of consent from the masses. So the ostensibly democratic State uses highly sophisticated techniques deployed through media, advertising, academic institutions, funding bribery, loading of the courts — *and constitutional powers* — to obtain popular legitimacy for otherwise inherently unpopular, even unjust, State programs.

Is this not thoroughly bizarre, given that the democratic State is supposed in its essence to be an expression of the people's will? Yet by far the largest consumer of advertising dollars in Canada is government. In 1992, our federal government spent $113 million on advertising, and the provinces and territories almost $91 million, for a grand total of almost $205 million.[12] In the same period, Canada's largest private advertiser was General Motors, at $105 million. I repeat: that's advertising, professional techniques used to change minds. If readers find they are unalarmed at such news, it can only be because they have already succumbed. As long ago as 1934, U.S. Senator Huey Long (who himself had a lot of dark experience using the machinery of government) warned that "when fascism comes to America, it will come in the name of democracy." The most prescient writer ever to have described this process of democratic pacification that precedes the rise of collectivism in formerly free societies, was Alexis de Tocqueville. In his 1840 essay, "Despotism in Democratic Nations," he wrote:

> After having thus successfully taken each member of the community in its powerful grasp and fashioned him at will, the supreme power then extends its arm over the whole community. It covers the surface of society with a network of small complicated rules, minute and uniform, through which the most original minds and the most energetic characters cannot penetrate, to rise above the crowd. The will of man is not shattered, but softened, bent, and guided; men are seldom forced by it to act, but they are constantly restrained from acting. Such a power does not destroy, but it prevents existence; it does not tyrannize, but it compresses, enervates, extinguishes, and stupefies a people, till each nation is reduced to nothing better than a flock of timid and industrious animals, of which the government is the shepherd.[13]

Both Canada and the United States have to date avoided most of the statist extremes, civil strife, and atrocities so sadly typical of most of the modern post-Christian European states in this century, whether directed against each other, or their own citizens. But the world is once again ripe for deadly conflagration sparked by a ready combination of power and righteousness. So we must pause to reflect, for seldom in the recent history of Canada and the U.S. — yes, Canada will be dragged along — have both nations so thoughtlessly flirted with collectivist justifications for the use of arbitrary power against their own citizens. In fact, Canada's most recent exercise in constitutional horse trading, the doomed Charlottetown Accord of 1992, was almost exclusively devoted, not to the defence of individuals against the State, but to debates over the privileges and powers of competing social and political collectivities.

It is the normalization of such arbitrary powers, *supported by constitutional documents* and the courts, and imposed on a nation's own citizens, that soon blinds and numbs them to the use of arbitrary powers against all others. The range of possible moral — and therefore political — options they are prepared to entertain becomes so narrow, and the range of expanded powers they deem legitimate so broad, that all arbitrary power soon seems normal. Then the egalitarian policy they thought was a shield, becomes a sword. Then, too late, they discover it was always a sword; first turned against themselves and their freedoms (the internal enemy), then outwards against others (some

23

external enemy). My hope is that by the end of this essay, readers will at least feel the sharp edge of that sword.

THE PARADOX OF DEMOCRACY

The unfolding and unfortunate logic of modern liberalism in the West (that the State now has an obligation to ensure not just equal freedom before the law, but the fruits of an equal life for all) has made acutely visible the same two ancient and inevitable paradoxes that have felled all previous egalitarian societies. First, "freedoms" and "rights" are contradictory notions, as are freedom and equality. Once you guarantee more of one, you are by implication guaranteeing less of the other. For instance, if government provides a subsidy to John, thus satisfying his economic right, it must take the money in taxes from Paul, thus reducing Paul's economic freedom. The right to so-called employment-equity jobs for women or blacks reduces the employment freedom of males and whites. Reduces? It positively launches the State into racist policies quite typical of collectivist states (as the socialist government of Ontario discovered in 1993 when one of its own well-publicized job advertisements openly barred applications from white males). On even more divisive moral matters, the right to a tax-funded abortion for Mary-Lou, for example, reduces the freedom of Sally-Ann, whose taxes cannot be legally withheld to protest something she opposes.

The second paradox is that egalitarian states justify their existence theoretically, by forced redistribution from high to low income

24

earners in order to maximize the satisfactions of the people as a whole. Yet satisfactions can only be maximized when buyers and sellers voluntarily trade what they want with each other, not what they are told to trade. It is a blatant inconsistency in theory for a state to intervene in the choices of the people in order to maximize their satisfactions by forcibly blocking their choices.[14] And so on.

The general result in a modern egalitarian democracy wherein politicians must ceaselessly strive for the popular vote is that the equal rights and freedoms promised to all are soon countered by policies and institutions designed to provide more rights to some groups of citizens than to others. This latter sort of official inequity, actually promoted as State policy in Canada's Constitution, is intended to eliminate the galling — ultimately, to the government, embarrassing — natural differences in status and performance that result from the natural choices of free human beings. Such a vote-balancing act by its very nature requires an increasingly anti-democratic grip on power, and such official Group Think is the founding basis of all forms of collectivism. The result, as the philosopher Bertrand de Jouvenel put it, is that "the more one considers the matter, the clearer it becomes that redistribution is in effect far less a redistribution of free income from the richer to the poorer, as we imagined, than a redistribution of power from the individual to the State." In this way democracy, based on a political philosophy that is inherently individualist, local, and anti-government, becomes egalitarian, centralist, and pro-government. In this way the most important political philosophy of the person ever conceived has been dangerously transformed.

DUMBING DOWN DEMOCRACY

O nce cornered by such logical and moral dilemmas, how is it possible for an ostensibly democratic government to justify the amount of anti-democratic power required to maintain itself? Through a class of elites expert in the marketing of power through ceaseless invocation of "the public interest" or "the public good." This Rousseau-style, guilt-inducing concept is used to legitimize a spreading web of State control over an often resistant, misled, and cynical public. Because more democratic control for the people ought to mean less power for the State, and not the reverse, all democratic power thus soon becomes self-contradictory. As mentioned, in a Canada that now has one government employee for every 5.5 citizens and the highest taxes in our history, we are demonstrably less free than ever before. So a third paradox is that to get more power in a democracy, politicians have to falsify their own democratic principles. To have a pure democracy, they would voluntarily have to put themselves almost entirely out of business. They would have to think of the people, democracy, and freedom before themselves and their jobs, which of course they will not do. This is the living lie and therefore the Achilles heel of all democracies. Even while advocating the public good, politicians vie for control of a deceptive apparatus of power that throws the philosophy of democracy itself into an endless task of intellectual and moral self-justification. For of course, practically speaking, under any system, policies are designed not for the *public* good, but for the *political* good; that is, for political success. An easy test of this is the answer to this question: If effective policies were good for the people but bad for governments, would they be implemented? Answer: unlikely. The welfare State, for example, is pronounced good for the people, is said to be a fundamental value that unifies them. But in fact, it is mostly good for those who gain power, jobs, and influence from it. For as history clearly shows, and as we are currently seeing in Canada, welfare States eventually ruin civil society, first through a kind of calculus of envy and moral despair, then financially through the tax system. This has been true since Roman times, as anyone who has read the history of the downfall of that empire will know. But it is very likely that the people, then and now, were already morally ruined when such statism was first introduced, or else they would never have accepted the blatant substitution of so many regulations and dependencies of all kinds for freedom, privacy, work, and diligence. At any rate, the Public Good is soon transformed into massive public debt that will be only vaguely remembered by our modern Neroes, snoozing away their retirement on gold-plated public pensions worth more than the people themselves could ever afford. This is the course Canada has followed since the 1960s. We will see below how the law of the constitution has been aggressively used by politicans and the courts as an instrument to assist in this dire process. But first let us look at the main kinds of law that shape our lives.

THE THREE KINDS OF LAW

When it comes to the kinds of law meant to guarantee or restrict the general rights and freedoms of individuals, there are three main types.*

Law From Rulers

Charter law, or "code law" (such as our own Charter of Rights and Freedoms), is upheld as the highest abstract legal ideal and is always written to take precedence over all other lower forms of law in the nation. It is intentionally made very difficult to alter by its "entrenchment" in a constitution, where it is meant to lie out of reach of all political parties. For it is thought to have a higher value than law made by mere representatives of the people. As one constitutional expert put it to me: "Who would you trust more, a Member of Parliament, or a judge?" I chose the MP, on the grounds that I could elect or reject him, but not the judge. Charter law, untouchable by the people and their parties, is thus inherently anti-democratic.

It seems, however, that in all nations governed by charter law, the code, however well-intentioned it may have been, eventually and insidiously mutates into a kind of rulers' law,[15] imposed at every level by courts that by their nature become politicized. In some nations, the courts actually become instruments of terror.

---

* *For this purpose, I am leaving out the many kinds of law designed for specific narrow purposes, such as maritime law, criminal law, equity law, administrative law, and so on.*

The charters of the French Revolution, Nazi Germany, and the former Soviet Union were glorious-sounding documents ringing with phrases about human freedom and rights. But they legitimized some of the most horrifying tyranny in the history of the world against the citizens of those states, millions of whom were officially classified as the "internal enemy." It was the legal courts of the land that carried out the sentences. This simply means that strive as you will to place the law above the reach of the people, it can still be captured by politically interested parties and then turned against the people. As I said, the shield becomes a sword. We are still babes at this business, but take heed. Canada has a huge variety of "rights" codes in every province of the land and many "tribunals" and courts staffed with unelected political appointees who are currently stridently dictating correct behaviour and levying heavy fines and sentences against private individuals and corporations. Ontario's recently withdrawn Bill 55, "An Act to Amend the Human Rights Code," was proposed by a "conservative" member of the Ontario legislature, and was designed to prevent citizens from saying, publishing, selling, or displaying anything that "ridicules" or "demeans" or "discriminates" against any other person or class of persons. It carried a maximum fine of $50,000. It was modelled on a British Columbia law that is now in effect. For the most part, the values and behaviours such laws are suppressing are those relating to the founding values of Canada, once so strongly based in political freedom, family rights and privileges, free enterprise and private property, and religious belief.

Law From the People

Statute law is law made by the people through their parliaments. Unlike code law, it may be created, modified, or abolished in a parliament of representatives democratically elected by the people, in whom all power theoretically is vested. In other words, it has the great virtue of flexibility. It responds to the will of the people, who control it and alter it (through their elected representatives) to meet changing times. If a law made one year is deemed bad the next, then let's get rid of it, or make a better one, goes the thinking.

Those of us fortunate enough to live in Anglo Saxon–based nations need reminding that this form of law got its start in northern Europe around A.D. 450 when, as legend has it, the Britons invited from the continent the armies of the Angle warriors Hengist and Horsa. Briton soon became Angleland, or England. The Angle form of government was remarkable. The Angles considered themselves a commonwealth of freemen who selected leaders and passed all laws based on the consent of the people. Power flowed up, not down, and all leaders were strictly limited in power as servants of the people. Theirs was a very effective form of people's law, or parliament.

There were many subsequent political setbacks for the English, caused by such as William the Conqueror, who in 1066 imposed a French form of code, or rulers' law, on the people. But the people eventually rejected this. Beginning with the Magna Carta of 1215, they managed to institute a true parliamentary system that has endured and evolved in England since the thirteenth century. Those who study the history of individualism, private property, and personal freedom in the West will find these matters strongly defended in the laws of England long before the European continent got wind of such novelties.

In the New World, Thomas Jefferson and the founding fathers of America were keenly aware of the Greek, and the Anglo-Saxon influence, and called for a renaissance both of those principles and — as a Judeo-Christian nation — of the ancient and quite similar Judaic principles of self-government outlined in the Book of Deuteronomy (1:15-17).[16] These powerful sources, historical and theological, underlie the principles and the appeal of democracy, particulary in the New World. There, until very recently, the very ideas of personal freedom, moral agency, and self-governance have been central. For those nations without such principles and ideals, democracy must remain an empty word.

But one simple thing is clear: charter law and statute law are in conflict, and democracy, purely conceived, can only support the latter, because only then can the laws flow from the people up, rather than from the leaders down.

Law From Real Life

Common law, or "real-life law," is law made in the courts. It is a body of legal precedents and principles derived from centuries of judicial wisdom developed in actual cases, often based on traditional, unwritten principles of the culture. For example, the notions that "a man's home is his castle" or that "possession is nine-tenths of the law" are customary principles upheld over so many centuries by the people, judges, and juries that they have become commonly accepted principles of law. The underlying standard is *stare decisis*, meaning "stand by what has been decided."

For even when a statute law says "no trespassing," for example, a common-law court judge must still decide whether a fellow racing across your property to save his cat from your dog; or a neighbour's tree branch growing over your fence; or a police officer entering your home with no warrant — actually constitute a case of trespassing. Only such concrete real-life judgements give force and effect to abstract legal words. Common-law courts do not make statutes, but rather develop juridical principles that form into a body of law. Anyone who has ever been to court will know just how the outcome of most cases hangs on the court's interpretation of seemingly innocent legal words. The faith implicit in the common-law system is that through it we will have available to us a long history of smart judges and juries who have handed down to us their well-considered thought, winnowed of error.

FROM THE CONCRETE . . .

In countries based on the English model, this struggle between individual rights and State rights and the proportionality between them has been worked out both in parliaments (by the people), and through actual case law in the courts (by real-life situations). The common law is by nature retrospective, and bound by wise traditions derived on a case-by-case basis, from which it departs with great reluctance. Change, under common law, is therefore slow and piecemeal, because *the common law has no program for the reshaping of society*, and wants none because of its underlying belief that civil society is an organic, spontaneous reality, and must remain so, to be alive. Such a society evolves within the law, not because of the law. In turn, this reflects a further underlying assumption that each individual soul is inherently unique and different from all others, and needs a field of freedom within which to live, dream, act. It is only within this field of freedom that individuals can become persons, or self-realized moral agents. The common law, wishing to protect the flourishing of such natural freedoms and differences, is therefore intentionally anti-utopian, and naturally conservative. Its greatness flows from its implicit insistence that society ought to be shaped by the people, not by the State, or by the courts, because both are institutions as likely to tyrannize the people, as to civilize them. Until recent times, charter law has played only a small part in English-style nations; Britain, in fact, still does not have a written constitution. Its revered constitution is mostly the accumulation of centuries of inherited custom and convention, and is proudly said to be "unwritten."

. . .TO THE ABSTRACT

E ver since the serious weakening of religious faith began during the eighteenth-century Age of Enlightenment, however, most of the modernized world has suffered from a deepening spiritual emptiness. In reaction, most modern nations have been easily seduced by one or another shining secular vision of human perfectibility. As if to achieve the promise of such visions, to fill the void, as it were, there was a veritable rush to create secular codes and charters designed to embody the highest principles for the human and social perfection of the species. In other words, once faith in the tablets of Moses was lost, nations rushed to create secular tablets. The thinking seems to have been that if a few glowing abstract rights could be enunciated clearly enough, then concrete social reality would conform to them naturally, as iron filings are drawn to a magnet. Continental — especially French — intellectuals waxed rhapsodic about the infinite possibilities of the centralized, rational, and scientific organization and control of human societies under such codes. At last, all human and social evils would be conquered; heaven on earth was finally within reach.

Suffice it to say that this aggressive and often bloody secular search for the earthly heaven was and remains profoundly anti-religious because its initial assumption is that human perfectibility, whatever that is, is possible. The great world religions, on the other hand, stress that only God can be perfect. Humans, who are less than God, are by definition forever imperfect. Secular political philosophies therefore intentionally ignore even the slightest suggestion of the existence of constants of nature, human nature, or moral life, opting instead for a relativistic, even revolutionary, pro-active stance in all things. For if everything is relative, then all may be changed by social action. All varieties of relativism and cultural determinism are promoted, the better to sieze upon political opportunities to manipulate culture in the interests of a utopian vision. Whenever such visions are inscribed in unchangeable charters, trouble is a-brewing.

IT BEGAN IN THE NEW WORLD

As it happened, the first modern nation to work out such a code was the United States. Less tradition-bound than the older European nations, America was founded on the simple idea of rejection — of the restrictive traditions, corrupt religion, and authority of the old world — coupled with the vision of a new, free, and equal society. In the New World there were fewer impediments to the creation and imposition of an abstract and revolutionary charter of rights. As D. H. Lawrence put it half a century ago, America was based on the idea of freedom *from* the bonds of the past, but it wallows today in civil despair because it knows not what that freedom is *for*. And the trenchant contemporary British critic John Gray observes that for the modern liberal, America is not so much a political nation as "a civil religion" that erupts into periodic conflicts between its willed utopian political vision and its inherited, and quite conservative, values. Not the flag, motherhood, and apple pie, but rather the flag versus the latter two. Heaven pulls in one direction, roots in the opposite.

At any rate, to further the kingdom of heaven on earth, America produced its Declaration of Independence from British rule on July 4, 1776, declaring, "We hold these truths to be self-evident... ". Shortly afterward, in 1787, it produced its Constitution. Meanwhile France, seething with a rapidly corrupted revolutionary fervour, quickly took inspiration from the bold American declaration and created her own Declaration of the Rights of Man and Citizen (1789). In the name of these new abstract principles — all common-law protections by then having been dispensed with — France proceeded to murder hundreds of thousands of her own innocent citizens before she fell under absolute dictatorship. Rousseau's General Will created the Revolution, the chaos, and then the need for a despot to embody that Will.

It was the extraordinarily powerful English writer and parliamentarian Edmund Burke who, in his *Reflections on the Revolution in France* (1790),[17] almost singlehandedly and in the face of much initial ridicule dissuaded the English nation from following the disastrous French habit of adoring abstract utopian ideals. The problem with such ideals, as he wisely put it, is that their very "abstract perfection [is] their practical defect." Why? Because those who control power strive also to control the interpretations of abstractly worded concepts in codes, the better to monopolize society with those codes.

But society, he warned, is not an abstract invention of any one person, generation, or code. It is a complicated, slowly growing, and carefully nurtured convention handed down gently to us for safekeeping from a long and considered history. It is a sacred partnership, "not only between those who are living, but between those who are living, those who are dead, and those who are to be born." This formed what he called "the great primaeval contract of eternal society." And Burke begged the English and French citizenry to resist any narrow and dangerous fascination with utopian ideals, or any attempt to invent all human society anew on a page of print. And he foretold the awful bloodshed of the French Terror and its so-called Committee of Public Safety, whose hunger for egalitarian success could only be satisfied by more guillotines.

In our own century, Walter Lippman, in *The Public Philosophy*, insisted that traditions are the public world to which our private world is joined. Traditions must be transmitted from old to young, in a seamless web of memory, for "men can know more than their ancestors did only if they start with a knowledge of what their ancestors had already learned . . . that is why a society can be progressive only if it conserves its traditions."

The revolutionaries, socialists, and other lovers of abstract principle, Burke said, have got reality upside down. They "pervert the natural order of things . . . by setting up in the air [in the code] . . . what ought to be on the ground" (in conventions, the common law). Such people "are so taken up with their theories about the rights of man, that they have totally forgotten his nature." And because liberty, when men act in groups, always becomes raw power, we ought first to guard against what men do with that liberty. The answer from history is dire, Burke warned, because, at the end, from the work of such rights lovers you see nothing but the gallows.

An even more trenchant view of the vicious effect of the rights illusion on civil societies was uttered in 1602 by Shakespeare's character Ulysses, in *Troilus and Cressida*. There, in a long poetical passage of extraordinary power and insight, Ulysses expounds on what happens when societies lose their sense of "degree," by which he meant their sense of the natural place of prudence and the inherited wisdoms of civil life, which cannot possibly conform to any abstract utopian theory. At the point when political strength becomes "lord of imbecility" and right and wrong lose their meaning,

> Then everything includes itself in power,
> Power into will, will into appetite;
> And appetite, an universal wolf,
> So doubly seconded with will and power,
> Must make perforce an universal prey,
> And last eat up himself.

Think of the French Revolution. Think of the wars conducted in the name of Marxist, Nazi, or Fascist Will to abstract social perfections. Think of the disastrous history of socialism in the world, the blood, the bodies, the human sorrow; think of the encroachments of the modern welfare State in the name of an abstract "public good." Think of today's strident demands from the media and academics for political correctness. Tribunals all over North America are rushing to control minds, words, ideas, even social "environments." Think of the failed Charlottetown Accord, that vile feast of interest groups scrapping at the trough. You can see how it all begins when claims to abstract group rights move quickly to a seizure of political influence and power to claim those rights. Unbridled power is then fed by political will, and from there the appetites of the strongest to satisfy their social vision lead the way, and we get the universal wolf that eats up itself.

II
—

A JUDICIAL CIVIL WAR

Our Choice: A Free Society Under a Just Law, or an "Equal" Society Under Corrupt Law

After **115 years as a free nation**, guided by representatives of her people enjoying a British-based *parliamentary sovereignty*, a people's law, Canada, too, succumbed to the international rights fever, and had imposed upon her by Prime Minister Trudeau the Charter of Rights and Freedoms of 1982. Alas, just like other charter-based democratic nations, Canada is now slowly and painfully learning that such imposed abstract principles have the unfortunate effect of incrementally weakening parliaments, undermining common-law precedents, and replacing people's law with rulers' law. Later

I will argue that such egalitarian charters are the greatest menace not only to individual freedoms, but to the organic health of society itself, and that in the case of Canada, the imposition of such a charter set the stage for revolt in Quebec, and thereby for the possible dissolution of the nation.

The moment an abstract charter, or code, is introduced as the supreme law of the land into a country whose legal system was previously based on parliamentary sovereignty and the concrete common law, an almost irreversible transformation takes place. Suddenly, all laws made by legislatures must either pass the test of conformity to the code, or be thrown out by the court. (This is a complete reversal of the meaning of parliamentary law, whereby a true parliament of the people can reverse, amend, or correct the decision of any court, if it so wishes.) Once aware of this "charter chill," legislators soon begin to think, "Why bother to make a law the people say they want, if it will not pass the test of the Charter?" Even worse, they go on snooze control: "Why bother to scrutinize the issues at all? Let's just wait and see what the judges think." At this point, democracy as an expression of the people and their laws, however imperfect, has ended. Suddenly judges, many unwillingly, are transformed into social activists. They have no choice but to wilfully attribute personal meanings to abstract legal words and codes that reflect their personal idea of what concrete social reality *ought to be*. Suddenly we get *judicial sovereignty*, a concept utterly alien to democracy. Overnight, an ancient framework of law that once reflected the lives of the people and their concrete values is transformed into an instrument for the propagation of the judges' abstract values.*

How, then, in an historically freedom-loving country, is this conflict resolved between the traditional freedoms of the concrete common law and the abstract principles of the Constitution imposed upon those freedoms? With great difficulty. A judicial civil war soon erupts. In both the U.S. and Canada, conservative jurists say the courts must rule according to the *original intent* of the written constitution. The more numerous liberal jurists say that because the purpose of a constitution is to ensure a good society, then reading modern, progressive meanings into old words — thinking of the written constitution as a *living tree* — is not only acceptable, but necessary. At this point, because the direction of social evolution no longer determined by the will of the people but by the will of the judges on the bench, myriad interest groups strive aggressively to "load" the courts with judges favourable to their political and social views. They also contrive to take over law schools and law reform commissions, granting mechanisms, editorial boards, academic faculties, and so on. This is a great danger to all democracies, and a process already far advanced in the West, whereby an invasion of largely

---

* *Canada's Charter of Rights and Freedoms contains a clause called the "notwithstanding clause" (section 33) that gives any province the right to pass a law that may contravene the Charter. It was anticipated that any use of the clause would be to further freedoms, not repress them. Parliamentary sovereigntists, such as this writer, see this clause as a good thing because it ensures that legislatures, right or wrong, rather than judges, have the final say on important matters of public policy. But judicial sovereigntists, who by their nature distrust*

tax-funded liberal intellectuals succeeds in co-opting formerly democratic institutions and using them not for the people, but against them.

In the results of poll after poll, in the U.S. and Canada, whether the subject is taxation, education, abortion, homosexual rights, religion, welfare, unemployment policy, criminal justice, or the family . . . we see that public policy is generally contrary to popular values.

Americans have at least some protection. Their Declaration of Independence sets the freedom tone by defending the existence and priority of natural rights such as "life, liberty, and the pursuit of happiness." In contrast, Canada's British North America Act (1867), sets the tone for statism in section 91 by citing as its chief aim "Peace, Order, and good Government." In large measure, the American tone and emphasis is on the guarantee of individual freedoms and rights — on *non-interference* — while the Canadian emphasis is on the role of government to *control* such rights. The American Constitution, like the British Magna Carta, was largely meant to *restrain* power and to destroy

---

legislatures, see the clause as a terrible constitutional blemish that erodes the absoluteness of Charter rights (in which they assume there can be no wrong).

It does. It favours the people, not the courts. At any rate, Quebec's unfortunate, repressive use of the clause to defend its French-only sign law certainly bolsters the judicial side in this debate. In practice, however, any use of the notwithstanding clause is so politically impractical and unpopular it remains only a minor means, for better or worse, to ensure parliamentary supremacy.

My argument is that it is better to have parliamentary sovereignty to make laws, good or bad, that the people may alter, than to place the law beyond their reach where it may be altered and imposed by judges, good or bad.

monopolies of whatever type. It is true that Canada's original Constitution, the British North America Act of 1867, also provided, in structure if not wholly in spirit, for a stern division of powers to prevent monopoly. And this worked very well for a century, until this wise precaution was intentionally circumvented by wily politicians specifically seeking to create a welfare State under a constitution that just as specifically forbade it.

HOW WILY POLITICIANS CIRCUMVENTED THE LAW OF OUR CONSTITUTION

The BNA Act provided — still provides — that Canada's provincial and federal governments may attend only to the matters assigned to their respective jurisdictions in the act (national matters for the federal government, and local matters for each provincial government). Each level of government must be fiscally responsible. Federal borrowing may be on the Public Credit of Canada (section 91), but provincial borrowing must be *only on the sole credit of each province* (section 92). The federal parliament may amend the Constitution only on matters within its own jurisdiction. In other words, by and large, provinces must create their own wealth, and live, and borrow, within their means. The framers created this wise formula to restrict both the imprudent growth of provincial governments, and the encroachment of central government upon the provinces. Most importantly, the federal government was not to reach into provincial affairs, such as health care, education, welfare, or the enforced use of languages, through the nation's constitutional document. The strict federal division of powers was intended by the founders to be a safeguard against democratic totalitarianism, or mob rule, or central intervention and control of local life and privacy.

How the Government's Hands Were Untied

But what has happened? All these things the Constitution forbids, we are now doing. Here's how. Beginning in the mid-1960s under Prime Minister Lester Pearson, and continued with a vengeance by Pierre Trudeau and all after him, Canada's federal government made a deliberate decision to circumvent these wise retraints of the Constitution.

Pearson did so initially by coercing Canadian provinces into a "universal medicare" scheme. He carried this out by by first setting up uniform federal standards to which each province would have to conform in order to avail itself of his offer to pay fifty percent of each province's costs — a subsidy he planned to generate by more heavily taxing all citizens directly, or by borrowing on their behalf on the federal credit (exactly what the Constitution was designed to prevent). Although the first matter to be so imposed was national health care, the rest, such as welfare, education, bilingualism, multiculturalism, and so on, soon followed in a similar format.

Narrowly defined, this was a "legal" but sneaky mechanism for the creation of a welfare State in all but name. For although it is true that Canada's federal government has involved itself in minor transfer payments of some sort ever since 1867, these were formerly always within the restrictions of the division of powers. Not so for Pearson and Trudeau. Their scheme was to generate massive federal subsidies in order to bribe the provinces to conform to national standards, in areas restricted by our own Constitution to provincial authority. It was a scheme utterly contrary to the spirit and intent of Canada's original Constitution.[18] It was a form of fiscal bribery that shifted *de facto* control over a whole variety of programs from the provinces, to central government; reduced provincial freedoms; and enabled most provinces (therefore most Canadians) to live well beyond their means by a form of proxy borrowing from future generations. (Parallel to this was a centralizing movement within each province implemented through "regional governments" and intensive regulation that massively shifted powers from local communities to provincial governments, thus creating ten welfare states within a larger welfare State.)

In 1982, by imposing his all but unamendable Charter of Rights and Freedoms on Canadians, Prime Minister Trudeau strapped them legally into the constitutional straitjacket of a full-blown welfare State he had already almost single-handedly created administratively. What we observe in the 1990s is the super-debt crisis, downloading, and fiscal gridlock typical of all such welfare States. With it, we see the inevitable effort by Ottawa to reduce its transfer subsidies, thus throwing costs back on the provinces which, in turn, will ask why they now ought to conform to any national standard, and therefore why they shouldn't develop, once again, their own distinct programs. All circles are round. We can be sure of only one thing as the country unwinds: the same politicians, interest groups, and hangers-on that rode the system up, will still be there, riding it down. It is the people who always pay.

Steering the Ship

Once the 1982 Charter was in place — it is more a chart, than a charter — it basically directed the courts of the State (who would now alone decide what "democratic" means), right from section 1, to engineer society according to an egalitarian vision, regardless of whether or not such State action might trample on the people's declared rights and freedoms. That is partly why Canada, although it started down the socialist road much later than the U.S., has become so much more rapidly and thoroughly socialized. Our highest documents have enabled and encouraged this trend of squelching personal freedom in the name of rights.

A tidy demonstration of this clash between the philosophy of freedom and the machinery of rights can be found in recent judgements by Canada's Supreme Court, which, as Canada's national newspaper aptly pointed out, "has declared its bias" (*Globe and Mail*, November 9, 1993). The court has maintained that Canada's constitutional guarantees of freedom do not apply equally to all individuals, even though the Charter's section 15(1) explicitly says they do. Rather, "the court says it will hear equality-rights cases according to which group the individual belongs to. Equity among groups has replaced equality among individuals." Individual freedom as a principle is gone. Now only egalitarian ratios between social groups count. Justice Bertha Wilson herself, a vigorous proponent of equality and therefore just as vigorous an opponent of freedom, admitted as much in the same article when she said "while Section 15 speaks in terms of a right to equality, it really addresses the problem of inequality." Unelected judges, and not the people's elected legislators, are to bring about the peaceable kingdom.

THE STRUGGLE CONTINUES

In *The Trouble With Canada*, I suggested that Canada, long a country based on English common-law traditions, yet with a large French cultural presence, is still struggling with the conflict between the English and French styles of government. For the English, or "bottom-up," style, is based on the notion that the most important political fact of life is individual freedom and responsibility and that there is a bundle of natural rights we all possess by virtue of being born humans. These cannot be given to a person, or taken away, by a charter, because they are inherent and pre-exist any such documents and indeed the whole idea of the State itself. Most importantly, the English view is that the rules of a constitution are a *consequence* of these pre-existing rights, are designed to protect them, and are not, as the French and other Europeans prefer, their *source*.[19] From these grow other important rights such as the right to the enjoyment of private property, free association, and so on.

NEGATIVE RIGHTS

It was people nurtured in the English style who were the first to entrench in the common law a clear legal and philosophical protection for such rights, and to argue for the creation of political institutions that would serve as checks and balances on the power of the State to erode them. Such rights are considered so inviolable or, as the Americans put it, "unalienable," that they are sometimes described as "negative rights" — their importance arising from our right *not* to be interfered with by others, particularly by governments. Each individual, in this view, is considered a moral agent who adds to or subtracts from the moral fabric of society by good or evil actions. The role of government in such a society is not to control the people and manage their morality but to create and then protect an environment in which they can manage it themselves, under the same rules for all. Moral direction under such a system arises not from any government — an institution to be largely distrusted — but from free civil society itself.

The economic effect of this style is the spontaneous development of a merit, or bonus system, in which voluntary economic activity — wealth creation — is allowed to flourish with minimal hindrance from the State and without intervention intended to control outcomes. The social effect is that free people operating under a common set of rules will always evolve a spontaneous society replete with a myriad of informal moral and social authorities, locally enforced by voluntary institutions such as family, church, school, corporation, club, and so on. Because so much voluntary informal authority exists in free and spontaneous societies, fewer formal laws and controls are necessary.

In contrast, the French, or European, style of government is collectivist, centralizing, "top-down," and rooted in the belief that people are not personally but only socially redeemable. The way to redemption is to create a virtuous society and keep anarchy at bay, not through individual moral agency but through the creation of a code, or charter, or constitution — a control document — imposed from above by a political elite. This process ensures that society is managed according to a pre-set idea of the social good, and also ensures a strong central government to supply the power. This is a quasi-utopian vision of society bent on social perfection, by force if necessary. It requires special legal immunities for public officials, unavailable to ordinary citizens, so the central plan for the people can be realized. For without such immunities, the people might legally resist. In retrospect, what all code-dominated nations are actually attempting to do (although they don't say as much) is to recreate the spiritual heaven in which they have long since ceased to believe, as a secular, materially satisfying realm here on earth. God may not have treated us all the same, goes the sentiment, but the State and its elites will.

The French style, however, seems inevitably to evolve into an unofficial two-class society, the governing elite and the governed, in which legislatures once adamantly democratic begin to see themselves not as carrying out the people's wishes but as shaping those wishes, and with increasing vigour marketing them back to the people along with the extensive apparatus required for their execution, and then entrenching the whole business in the code as rights. For if you want to create an egalitarian collectivist State — the only kind that requires big government — you must at a minimum entrench in the code a right to equal material benefits for all. After all, it is only from a mass of equalized individuals that one can expect a mass of allegiance. If you give them all the same things, they will pay you back by voting in the same way, is the logic. From this normalized notion of forced equality flows every other aberration of modern democracy.

How Individual Rights
Soon Become State Rights

At this stage, the die is cast. Instead of a mechanism designed to protect free citizens against the invasions and depradations of the State, such charters are soon transformed into enabling documents for the State's own activist and judge-led social-engineering program. Either the State, as in Canada, has been brazen enough to give itself specific rights to eradicate the natural differences between free human beings by engineering society through Charter-supported affirmative action and redistribution programs or, instead, as in both Canada and the U.S., the political, bureaucratic, academic, and legal systems become top-heavy with activist tribunals, scholars, and judges all eager to "read into" the abstract words of a whole variety of codes meanings that were never intended.

Unfortunately for free societies, the unintended consequence of enshrining a cornucopia of egalitarian rights and benefits in a code is always the barely perceptible but ultimately deadly weakening of self-reliance; a depression of the wealth-creating instincts of the people through the removal of incentives and the spurring of envy; and in general the slow transformation of a merit system into a handicap system in which equality of social outcomes, mostly through massive transfers of wealth from the productive to the unproductive, takes precedence over — in fact requires the suppression of — the very individual and economic freedoms promised by the code in the first place!

POSITIVE RIGHTS

Slowly, in place of the negative rights common to the English system since the thirteenth century, new "positive rights" (thus termed because they have specific concrete benefits in mind) are quickly invented and organized by an astonishing variety of interest groups, and forcibly inserted into charters and codes at every level as claims that the government promises to honour (the better to get itself re-elected). Such positive rights are provided without regard to effort or merit. And because they can only be provided by the State's first taking from some to give to others, these new rights, derived from abstract words, soon form a legal basis for a sort of handicap system, just as the concrete common law formed the basis for the merit system. The handicap system common to all welfare States seeks to equalize everyone fiscally by reducing the economic advantages (handicapping) of those with more income and transferring it to those with less. (We have seen that what it mostly does is transfer power to itself.)

From this point on, the State, instead of telling us what we cannot do, begins to use the law imperatively to force us to behave in certain ways, the better to fulfil the State's own egalitarian vision, and need for power. Canada's widespread use of racial and gender employment categories and exclusions, coercive language laws, coercive health system laws, pension laws, omnipresent taxation, and generally its myriad systemic nationwide programs for economic and social regulation and redistribution, are the manifestations of this process.

INHERENT FREEDOM VS. CONFERRED FREEDOM

A modest prediction: No people will ever free itself from unwarranted State power until it understands some important distinctions, such as between *prohibitive* law and *imperative* law, vigorously accepting the first when reasonable, and just as vigorously rejecting the second in principle. For in a curious way, our Charter of Rights and Freedoms has made us less free. As it happens, the first kind of law is typical of common law–based nations, the second typical of charter-based nations.

And what is the crucial difference between these two forms of law? Prohibitive laws are based on the assumption that each and every citizen is born naturally, *inherently*, and boundlessly free. His freedom is his own and may be used in any way he pleases as long as the law is not broken. The State does not tell him what to do, but rather, prohibits him from doing certain specific acts. A law such as "keep off the grass," for example, simply specifies that we may not walk on this particular bit of grass, but does not try to control or comment on our freedom to walk elsewhere.

Human freedom under this concept is like a light glowing within each individual soul. It is not a property that can ever be given or taken away from us by a third party, nor can it be qualified by a third party. Only the use of it may be qualified or properly restricted by prohibitive laws (which the people, in turn may alter if they wish). And we should clear up a common misconception: this quality of inherent human freedom is not diminished one whit by a person's being in jail; only the practical use of it is temporarily restricted.[20]

This has been the tremendous contribution of the Judeo-Christian West to political theory: that human freedom is a moral quality, and not a physical thing. And this points us to the great practical error indulged and promoted by all socialist thinkers. They strive to convert the moral *quality* on which freedom depends into a material *quantity*.[21] They see other people as inanimate things living in one or another kind of material prison that they say negates freedom, and so they strive to remove the prison via tax-funded social programs, "education," and the like, after which they assume the person inside will live in beautiful moral freedom, like themselves. The implication is that men are not free unless they are prosperous. But the high virtue of freedom, properly conceived, is that it is untouched by our condition in life, and persists as the cornerstone of our moral vision and of our perception of the totality and the possibilities of life itself, regardless of our immediate and changing circumstances. It is quite likely due only to the presence of this vision that we struggle to escape from, or to strive for any particular human condition. And it is unlikely that a democracy can survive for long unless this understanding of freedom as the key to moral agency is held as an absolute value.

Therefore it is surely by definition insulting when a government charter — created in secrecy by paid public servants, for heaven's sake — suddenly descends from on high to declare that henceforth we, the people, are "free," or that something we have done all our lives is now a "right" blessed by government. Only a snivelling species of people — or a very tired people — would take that lying down. After all, I say: I was born free, and the natural freedom of all human beings *precedes* the existence of any government. We, the people, therefore require our government to protect that freedom, primarily by abstaining from any qualification or definition of it. In other words, we expect the government to refrain from imperative laws that tell us what we must do, how to act, to behave, to think, who to hire, what to pay them, what to charge for our services, where to work, or live, and so on.

So how is it that the government suddenly acquires a right to *confer* a freedom on us by the simple act of handing us a small piece of paper, like a warden handing us our daily ration of bread? Very simply, it decides to appropriate the rights and freedoms we already have, by declaration, and then turns around and publicly bestows them upon us, then promises to *guarantee* them. Such words are dangerous. For as the great constitutional scholar A. V. Dicey put it, they suggest "the notion that personal liberty is a special privilege insured . . . by some power above the ordinary laws of the land. This is an idea utterly alien to English modes of thought, since with us freedom of person is not a special privilege but the outcome of the ordinary law of the land enforced by the Courts."[22] Nevertheless, in this sneaky way, presto! An inherent personal freedom that we ourselves formerly controlled is suddenly under the control and definition, and therefore under the limitation, of government. The whole concept and control of human freedom is thus transferred from the private to the public domain.

But why should we ever feel that our freedom is somehow more valuable because it has been blessed by our own paid servants? Can we not see the danger here, that *a freedom officially granted by the State is a freedom that may just as officially be redefined, revoked, or suspended?* Alas, once having accepted the deception that this precious quality of our personal lives *derives* from the State, we are too weak to protest whenever freedom is officially abridged, as it is, daily, in minute ways. Since the advent of the Charter, we now have a specific, limited number of narrowly defined abstract freedoms, and such freedoms now form our fetters, for to travel outside those definitions we must ask unelected judges to tell us whether, in doing so, we will still be free.[23]

Tellingly, the evolution of all modern democracies has been away from prohibitive and towards imperative law. Away, that is, from general rules of conduct and general principles, towards arbitrary authoritarian law, sanctioned by the highest institutions of government, and intended specifically to coerce and control the behaviours of private individuals and groups and the outcomes of society.

CAN THESE CONFLICTING STYLES MIX?

Despite Canada's brave efforts ever since Confederation in 1867 to blend these two styles, they are inherently incompatible, even mutually destructive. This is Canada's predicament. Ever since the battle of the Plains of Abraham, in 1759, there has been a national struggle for supremacy between these conflicting visions (as there has been with varying degrees of emphasis in all democracies, ancient and modern). And in 1982 we actually entrenched this centuries-old philosophical conflict within our highest legal document. The situation is now like that confronting a sculptor of plaster. If he knows exactly what he wants to make, he can finish the whole thing nicely before it hardens. But if he doesn't, the plaster hardens halfway through, and he's stuck with the quixotic result. From then on, he can only chip little bits away, or stick other bits on to make the whole thing look more acceptable. The fiasco of the Charlottetown Accord, a government deal decisively slain by plebiscite in October 1992, was just another in a long series of expensive constitutional plastering jobs.

HOW DID IT HAPPEN?

We have seen how after Canada had flourished for generations under English-style rule, modern liberals (I mean those interested in imposed positive law, egalitarians) came to power in 1968, and assisted by like thinkers from many other parties, began to change everything. While English Canada slept, they swiftly transformed the country into a more French-style nation. They imposed the machinery of a vast centralizing bureaucracy, encouraged a myriad of crown corporations (from fifty in 1965 to more than a thousand by 1984), imposed a national program of bilingualism (remember, as a nation Canada has never been bilingual, and will never be); and saddled us with an abstract code, our 1982 Charter with its socialist redistributionist dogma. Prime Minister Trudeau was well aware that the Charter would be in immediate and inherent conflict with the British common-law tradition. When asked early in his career "What society would you choose to make Canada?" he answered, "Labour-party socialist — or Cuban socialism, or Chinese socialism."

In legal terms, Trudeau's Charter was the top-down code system of law smothering a bottom-up common-law and parliamentary system. Ultimately, as future generations who will have to pay for all this will see in utterly stark economic terms, it was the handicap system smothering the merit system, and therefore all the values underlying it. It was also the declaration of the priority of the State's social vision as expressed through the State's courts and appointed judges, tribunals, and commissions — the whole quasi-governmental apparatus — over the social vision of individual citizens, their families, and their elected representatives. It was the replacement of people's law with rulers' law. For although Canada's Charter ostensibly defends the individual against the State, it in fact presupposes the huge intervening State required to satisfy all the uniform positive rights to goods and services guaranteed by the Charter itself, the disastrous effects of which on this formerly free and fiscally sound nation are at last sharply visible in our crushing total national debt.*

The various constitutional "crises" that arose after 1982 — the failed Meech Lake Accord, the defeated Charlottetown Accord of 1992, and the public opposition between the separatist Bloc Québécois and the Reform Party (which says no more pandering to Quebec or any other province) in the 1993 federal election — were active symptoms of this underlying conflict. We need to understand as a nation that just as Quebec prefers its own "distinct" centralism, for reasons arising from the history of French thought, English Canada, for reasons arising from the history of English thought, will always reject anything but political equality among provinces. More crises will arise because as a people we have not even begun to address the conflicting root principles, nor even attempted to answer the most basic questions, such as, *What is a constitution, anyway?*

---

* *Readers will see this most easily in the many charts printed in the author's two books,* The Trouble With Canada *(Stoddart, 1990, revised edition, 1994), chapter seven; and* The War Against the Family *(Stoddart, 1992), chapter six. As of January 1994, Canada's total cumulative debt, comprised of federal, provincial, municipal, and crown corporation debt, and including the totality of Canada's unfunded pension liabilities, came to about $1.1 trillion dollars, or about $125,000 per taxpayer.*

III

THE REAL THING

A Constitution Is About Rules, Not Deals

A **true constitution is a set** *of conventional rules and general principles by which the people and their various levels of government are allowed to make their deals; but it must never, in itself, be a deal.*

Well, by this standard, it is easy to see that Canada's repeated "constitutional" failures arise because we have not been discussing a true constitution, or set of rules of just conduct, equal for all. We have been discussing deal-making, which is destined to fail because such deals — a kind of political horse trading — attempt to enshrine permanent political solutions to the temporary and changing social and economic grievances of an endless stream of warring interest groups all straining at the public trough: feminists, natives, homosexuals, unionists, lobbyists, welfarists, bilingualists, francophones, anglophones, visible minorities, multiculturalists, lawyers, business groups, and the various sub-groups of these, broken down further by gender, language, colour, and so on. It's a disgusting and shameful spectacle unworthy of a great people.

THE SHAMEFUL DETAILS

Specifically, Canada's Charlottetown Accord (October 1992) was a matrix of conflicting "deals" between various governments, provinces, and interest groups. It included a deal to fix Quebec's parliamentary representation at twenty-five percent forever, regardless of Quebec's (declining) share of national population; a deal to create aboriginal homelands with a third level of government, and the concept of the right to inherent native self-government, thus constituting what Vancouver journalist Trevor Lautens described as "affirmative apartheid"; a deal permitting quota senate representation based on gender, race, language, and the like; a deal to entrench official bilingualism and multiculturalism coast-to-coast forever; a deal to enshrine Quebec as the first among provinces under a "distinct society" status; a deal to grant Quebec three of nine Supreme Court justices forever, regardless of population; a deal allowing Quebec (only) to appoint, rather than elect senators; a deal for a "double majority" vote for Quebec senators (only) — effectively a right to a veto — on all Canadian cultural policy that might be deemed in any way to impact on Quebec; a deal to provide all

Canadians equal rights (paid for by the tax system) to a high standard of living through a cornucopia of "free" (pre-paid) medical, educational, food, housing, and environmental services. This last was most pernicious of all, for it sought *to convert the idea of freedom into the idea of material security*, a commodity, thus debasing morality itself. The words "equality," "equal," or "equalization" appeared in this document twenty-three times; the word "authority" eight times; the word "liberty" — not at all.

In contrast, in the original seven articles of the U.S. Constitution, and again in the U.S. Bill of Rights, the word "no," *used as a direct restraint on government*, occurs thirty-three times.[24]

DOES A CONSTITUTION BELONG TO THE PEOPLE, OR TO THE GOVERNMENT?

All constitutional experts agree on at least one thing. Unless the bulk of a constitution reflects and is supported by a moral consensus of the people, it lacks legitimacy. In this sense, all Canada's recent so-called constitutional exercises have been illegitimate. The 1982 Charter of Rights and Freedoms was imposed on Canadians by a single citizen, with the help of nine provincial premiers, *none of whom had the slightest mandate from the people* to change this nation's most important document. And the tenth, Quebec's premier René Lévesque, who did have such a mandate, was effectively eliminated from the process! The failed Meech Lake Accord, which would in fact have had the salutary if tortured effect of somewhat decentralizing Trudeau's machinery, was created by the same high-handed, to-hell-with-the-people process. And the people let the government know! So the 1992 Charlottetown Accord experience was, well, a little different... With a loud crashing noise, Canada's elites, from out-of-touch politicians, to half-educated media, to snooty academics, got their comeuppance when, in October 1992, Canadians issued a bracing repudiation by plebiscite of the government's Charlottetown Accord (by then mockingly relabelled by many the Charlatan Accord).

For the truth is that at no previous time had the Canadian people ever before been asked to create or accept or amend a proposed constitution, unlike, say, the Swiss, Australians, or Americans, who at least have had some say on the terms of their most cherished legal document. Canada's constitutional charades are, however, a classic example of the government versus the people. The reason this is so, we are left to surmise, is that true instruments of direct democracy — such as recall, binding referendums, and citizen initiatives (explained below) — enjoyed with particular energy by the Swiss, *prevent the political class from structuring society against the interests of the people*, from taxing them to death, and from spending their money in unrestricted ways. And it is true the very same instruments could allow a simple majority of the people to trample individual rights, thus engendering the worst nightmares of democratic mob rule. But modern electorates want these instruments not so much to govern as to reduce and discipline government. So under an elitist government, every effort is made to avoid such instruments. Inquiries are held, royal commissions are struck, standing committees and task forces established. But none of these constitutes a device with any legal power over the government which, with predictable regularity, shelves, forgets, or simply dismisses all the findings. Poor fools that we are, all of these devices are in reality the opposite of democratic: they are bureaucratic strategies for diffusing popular dissent.

It is a truism, as remarked earlier, that all pure democracies tend to commit suicide because majority interests quickly set about to dominate the political process, and eagerly trample the rights and freedoms of the forty-nine percent. The whole purpose of a *rule of law*, of a *division of powers* in a federal State, and of built-in *checks and balances* on power, is to establish an institutional *design* that prevents this mob seizure of the political *process*, while still promoting democratic expression.

So let us now consider briefly what a true constitution ought to be, not in detail, but in terms of the general values and principles of a free and responsible society.

1. *Citizens Only*

A constitution should be blind to any differences between people, or groups. It must speak only of "citizens," without qualification, all of whom are subject to the same rule of law.

The underlying conviction of such a system is that all free nations must have *a government of laws, and not a government of men*. In other words, proper laws, applied equally to all, regardless of their station in life, are far preferable to a government changing the laws to suit the purposes of government.

Canada's current Charter fails this test, for it contains numerous sections — notably 1 and 15(2), which are "affirmative action" clauses — intentionally designed to permit the State to treat *whole groups* of citizens differently, according to language, sex, religion, ability, or ethnicity — or to degree of "disadvantage," in order to correct past "injustice" (for which dead predecessors are deemed guilty), thus to create equal results for all (by disadvantaging innocent living citizens). A contemporary white man of the highest credentials may be denied university entrance, for example, because some sanctimonious modern liberal tribunal believes his great-great-great-grandfather was guilty of racism. Thus do modern collectivists, spurred by arrogant convictions of their own moral purity, embrace the phantasmagorical notion that they are judges of all the human good and evil in history.

But because many very real individual, occupational, sexual, cultural, moral, racial, intellectual, or behavioural differences spring from real personal, historical, or biological sources, or choices, such constitutional clauses are a surefire invitation for all those who differ from each other to form a political interest group and fight for a higher "constitutional ranking" to gain some advantage, or just to obtain the highest victim status. But I say it is better to have a free society under a just law, than an equal society under a corrupt law.

2. No Constitutional Ranking

As mentioned above, Canada's Constitution "ranks" people according to language (special privileges for French — and English — speakers, but not for others), gender (women are given attention, men are not), race (aboriginal peoples are sin-gled out for attention, but not others), religion (Roman Catholics get public funding, other religious groups do not), and a few other categories, too. If we want a free society under a just rule of law, equal for all, all this must be trashed. Our Charter actual-ly goes so far as to specify that if you live in Quebec, you may not educate your children in English, unless you were yourself educated in English. But the same rule for French does not apply to French Canadians elsewhere in Canada. This is justice?

3. A Rule of Law

No truly democratic state can survive for long without a firm rule of law. A good constitution must include the concept of a set of *general laws and principles* equally applicable to all citizens, with *no exceptions* for public officials or government itself. This con-cept of equality before the law was the crowning achievement of English classical liberalism (since abandoned by modern liberals). It specified that *there shall be no arbitrary rule* (such as may still be found in virtually all European constitutions). All shall be treat-ed the same. The idea of official exemption from the ordinary laws of the land for public officials, so commonly accepted in countries such as France, is called the *droit administratif*. It means that a public official on government business may with impunity do such things as seize your personal or business documents without a warrant, officially discriminate against you or your children, or, in the case of Canada, haul you before a language tribunal, or a human rights tribunal, where, contrary to our Constitution, you are presumed guilty until proven innocent. And you are not legally permitted to sue the government or these officials.

But as A. V. Dicey put it, similarities between the French and English systems "must not conceal the fact that *droit administratif* still contains ideas foreign to English convictions with regard to the rule of law . . . ."[25] And again: "This idea is utterly unknown to the law of England, and indeed is fundamentally inconsistent with our traditions and customs."[26] Currently, Canada's Constitution badly fails the rule-of-law test, because it specifically orders the State to take from some to give to others, as a form of differential justice. And the Charter itself is a general licence for governments to trample the freedoms of the people in the name of a long-standing collectivist principle: the State may legally discriminate, but individuals and employers may not. The State is always right. Remember fanatics like Mussolini. All right and goodness flows from the State at the top. But I say the mere existence of such clauses in our Charter institutionalizes immorality in the nation's highest legal document. We have yet to understand that the plain reason our Charter contains two different standards of law — one for the rulers, one for the people — is that *otherwise the people could legally resist* intervention and control by the State. But the State does not want resistance, so it makes its own immoral acts legal. And the people continue to sleep.

4. *Basic Freedoms Must Be Protected*
A good constitution must at a minimum protect:

i) *Personal Freedom*, which means it must protect the notion of inherent personal freedom and responsibility limited only by prohibitive law, and it should further insist that any government actions beyond those required of a minimal State (protection of all citizens against force, theft, fraud, enforcement of contracts, and so on) *are morally unjustified.*

ii) *Free Speech*, which means the right of citizens to freely express and publish their ideas. In its origins the concept of "free speech" refers mostly to intellectual, political, philosophical, and religious matters — argumentation — and does not imply a right to breach local moral standards: to walk naked in the street, for example, or sell pornography to children. Over such matters, citizens ought to have powerful local control. But under a charter, they do not and cannot possibly have local control *because a specific objective of all charters is to overrule local control* in the name of the all-knowing State and replace it with a uniform national standard (Rousseau's General Will).

And where will this standard come from? From political elites who invent it and then entrench it in the charter, with its interpretation controlled by legal activists. Here is the danger: because all collectivist regimes, all forms of parliamentary socialism, regardless of how mild or tyrannical, must ensure the broadest voting base possible, their inherent practical interest lies in *the neutralization of all local moral standards* that might permit citizens in different locations to be treated differently. The local community law in Kamloops, B.C., that wants to deny citizens the right to rent sadomasochistic sex videos will be struck down by the Charter because a community in Ontario, say, allows them to be sold. Immediately, from the ramparts, the cry goes up, "That's discrimination under the Charter. If they can see them, why can't we?" But beware. Because the democratic State always wants more vote support, the trend in moral and sexual matters is never to deny, always to permit; never to ask for control, which is difficult, always to permit release and self-expression (Rousseau, again: we are basically good, so self-expression is to be encouraged). Just as stringently, personal expression opposing State policies and laws must be discouraged (correctness). That is why you may buy hard-core pornography at the local video store, but you may not openly promote your religion, or speak publicly against things like homosexuality. You will be deemed a discriminator, who prefers one kind of behaviour over another. Thus do all national standards in moral matters tend towards the lowest, not the highest, common denominator. That is why nations that permit a great deal of local control over moral matters are always conservative, while democratic nations of the welfare-State type, generally become morally slack and permissive. For it is much easier for government to please people and their appetites, than to deny them. (It is different for the totalitarian nations. Because they do not have to please voters, there is no *quid pro quo*. That is to say, there is nothing the State must exchange with the people, like sexual licence, to get their sheepish obedience.)

iii) *Fair Trial*, which means that even those accused of the most heinous crimes are innocent until proven guilty, and have a right to due process of law, regardless of their station in life. Kings and beggars must, for the same crime, receive the same justice and the same punishment.

iv) *Property Rights*. Canada's Constitution does not specifically protect the right of citizens to own and enjoy property (although our common law does). The justified fear is that unless the Constitution supports this common-law right to own and enjoy private property, this right — without which the whole concept of freedom is diminished — will be increasingly eroded in any test under the Charter. For history shows that many states that allow citizens the right to own property, so heavily regulate its use that ownership becomes almost meaningless — there is in fact no enjoyment of property. And without the possibility of the common man owning and enjoying his own property, freedom has no physical manifestation. He has not motive to buy or sell, nor even make a teaspoon he is not allowed to own. So he does nothing. Most important of all, without a clearly protected right to private property, he cannot keep the State out of his home or office, or even from opening a private letter. It is the constitutional protection of private property that in turn protects us against the prying State. Such rights in Canada are not only unprotected but have been seriously eroded ever since the 1960s. We will learn, too late, that as the rights of private property and the right of privacy die, freedom dies.

And we must take care never to forget a sobering lesson from history. The underlying argument all socialists rely on to nationalize, regulate, and outlaw private property is that they want to eliminate wealth differences and therefore frictions between people, in the interests of a peaceful, communal bond. And yet every nation that has banned private property for this reason is characterized instead by the pervasive presence of repression and the police control of private life. Nothing peaceful and communal here. Throughout history, and with few primitive exceptions, the freedom to own private property is inversely related to the growth of the police State.[27]

The reason is interesting. When people own property, they determine their own futures through proper care and nurture of everything they own. They create future-oriented responsibilities and duties, both financial and moral, that inexorably connect them and their offspring to the outcomes of family effort in the tangible material world surrounding them. Their future is concrete and real, not some abstract utopian promise. In such a world, there is little need for internal police, because the people largely police themselves through their common concerns and respect for each other's property.

In a socialist State, however, the reverse holds true. Because nothing belongs to anybody, everything is open to abuse, especially public property (all property, in such a State). All property therefore soon becomes for the citizenry a symbol for the hated, oppressive State itself. So there is little self-control, much abuse, and therefore many police.

Finally, the constitution of a free society must contain a "takings" clause that guarantees fair-market compensation, under due process, for any property appropriated for public use (taken) by the State. Ours does not, for the reason that there was really no need for our leaders to give us a Charter right to compensation for property that we do not have a Charter right to own.

v) *Free Trade*. The economic right of all citizens to trade their goods and services voluntarily between themselves and their regions, without impediment or tariff, must be guaranteed. But Canada is awash in trade barriers, regulations, centralized marketing boards, and State monopolies of all kinds, which directly and indirectly interfere with free-market principles and processes. Canada ought to scrap all this and declare itself constitutionally committed to the economic right of free trade between all citizens and regions, and outlaw all internal taxes, tariffs, and monopoly privileges.

One thing is clear: all tariffs and trade barriers tend to protect and favour producers, who, either through lobby groups, contributions, or such things as union vote power, in turn protect and support the government, regardless of party. Parties vie for this plum. But all truly free trade, while it may hurt some who have relied on protections, is essentially designed to favour the consumer — the people. (The North American Free Trade Agreement, while an advance, is really a producers accord. It is a 700-page book of regulations, with 700 additional pages of regulatory specifications and rules designed to favour producers.)

5. *Language*
A free country ought to aim for a free market in languages, without restraint or coercion by the State. Provinces that wish to have

an "official language(s)" for public affairs may regulate this matter internally, and territorially, by referendum, as local need dictates. There ought to be no such thing as a "portable" language right carried by citizens personally wherever they travel in the country. The notion of forcing the citizens to pay for a bilingual French-English sign deep in the forest of some remote provincial park in, say, British Columbia (a province whose unofficial second language is Chinese), under threat of fines and jail sentences, is bizarre. The idea of forcing businesses in Quebec to post their signs in French, and outlawing English, is, well, totalitarian.

Currently, Canada as a whole, and Quebec in particular, have the most oppressive language laws, tribunals, and interventions in the free world.

6. *No Social Engineering*

A constitution must forbid social engineering by the State designed to equalize citizens, economies, or regions. Rather, it should guarantee the freedom of citizens to migrate to those regions to express their personal or economic aspirations and differences in any fashion they choose within the law. There should be no constitutional promises of transfer payments or benefits to any person or region, nor recognition of any claims for goods or services. Instead, Canada pays hundreds of thousands of citizens to remain in parts of the country where there are no jobs, and (under the present system) never will be any jobs.

And it does not matter if some provinces are rich and some are poor. Let the chips fall where they may. We should not set up our Constitution as a document that determines personal or material satisfactions. Neither should we tell our young children that when they grow up, someone else will owe them a living. Neither should our citizens be told this. In fact as a general guideline I would say that any principle we cannot honestly teach our children should not be put in a constitution. To do so is to extinguish the living flame of the family, which in turn burns at the living heart of the community.

7. *Restraint*

A good constitution must be a powerful instrument for the protection of the people, their freedoms, families, and enterprises — their entire society — *from the depradations and interventions of the State itself*. In it must be carefully spelled out the basis of the minimal State, and for the specific systems for restraining, balancing, and checking the powers of government, which must be thoroughly characterized as the servant of the people, and obedient to their duly expressed will.

Earlier, I said that a pure democracy — if such a thing can even be imagined — is itself a danger to civil society, because an impulsive majority, or one captured and cajoled by interest groups, could simply run roughshod over forty-nine percent of the people, trampling the civil rights of individuals. Quebec is ripe for this, as we shall see. So the checks and balances of a good federal system must be designed to act as a kind of brake against the impulsivity of the people, and of parliament itself. In fact, the beauty of a truly federal (as opposed to centralized) system is that it forces democracy to operate locally, rather than nationally, in the foreknowledge that when operated nationally, local desires and morals are soon crushed.

8. Representation

That is why the people must be fairly represented by population in an elected parliament, but equally by province in an elected upper chamber, or senate, the prime function of which is to check the impulsivity of parliament.

The original idea for an unelected Senate was to ensure that mob rule could not easily take over through democratic means and trample minority rights. That is still a good argument. However, because the current Senate is widely perceived to be corrupted through political patronage, it would seem that placing it on an elected basis may be the only way to restore some balance. The fear of an elected Senate would then be: What federal institution, in the name of high principle, could possibly block mob rule or collusion between Commons and Senate? There would be only the courts. And they are now slaves to the Charter. Writer John Robson suggests that if the Senate is to be elected, then let it be by provincial legislature, and on a staggered-term basis, so that the design of the Senate blocks collusion by parties (it would then be almost impossible to assemble a single-party majority in both houses at once).[28]

In a free society the constitution must also ensure that parliament retains its sovereignty over the courts, so that the elected parliament (the people), and not a group of politically appointed judges, or influential interest groups, will always be the final maker of the laws. The prime function of the Supreme Court must then be to adjudicate the laws (not to make them or to "read into" them) — in order to balance the divided rights of provinces, or states, as against the federal government. In addition, when political representatives are unresponsive, a sure mechanism for amendment of the constitution by the people themselves must be in place.

9. *Only Negative Rights*

A good constitution will specify that the State must not interfere with the natural inherent rights and freedoms of individuals. It will specifically say that it is the role of government to guarantee equality before the law, which, for example, shall treat a rich man and a pauper with the same severity — but not to guarantee equality of material things to anyone. For to do so is to confuse freedom with security. And to promise security to some is to guarantee slavery to others. It is to turn this precious moral quality of the human being and of human societies into a legislatable commodity for manipulation by governments, tax policies, subsidies, transfers, and worst of all, by constitutions themselves. There must be no positive rights or benefits guaranteed.

10. *Subsidiarity*

This is an ancient term meaning that in a free society all emphasis shall be on localism, not centralism. Because the glory of free societies arises from the free moral agency of the citizens, the political environment must encourage the maximum use of moral agency in personal, family, and community life, and desist from policies designed to relieve human beings from the necessity of solving their own problems. Under the rule of subsidiarity, all problems must be solved at the level where they originate, and a higher level of government invoked only if a lower fails. Switzerland has such a clause in its constitution to encourage local resolution of needs and conflicts, which is good for the people, and to discourage national, homogenizing solutions, which are only good for political parties and bureaucrats.

Perhaps the finest effect of subsidiarity is that it results in competition between governments to please the people. This is also one of the highest gifts of federalism to democracy. Governments that overtax or overlegislate will be punished because people will migrate to other competing jurisdictions (just as businesses do now to provinces or countries that treat them better). Centralism eliminates competition between governments and exposes the people to a suffocating taxing and regulating monopoly. Sound familiar?

11. *True Federalism*
A good federal constitution must provide that the separate states or provinces are united (a sovereign nation of sovereign provinces) only by a limited number of well-defined federal duties to which all pledge themselves. Seven basic federal ministries (Justice and Police, National Defence, Interior, Finance, Economic Affairs, Transport and Energy, Foreign Affairs) will serve the purposes of any federal government, regardless of size. The secret to a successful federation is that it *divides* the powers, and thus forces each

smaller entity to cope with its own means and by its own lights, *restricting* the human centralizing impulse at the outset. In a good federal union, the so-called "residual powers" — anything else that may arise but which has not been delegated by the constitution — must be left in the hands of the provinces and their communities (thus forcing subsidiarity). Unfortunately, Canada's current Constitution gives residual powers, and ultimate control over all provincial laws, to the federal government (which explains in part why our federal government has had uncontrolled growth).

12. *Direct Democracy*

Three instruments are required, not so much so that the people can rule directly at every turn — they are too busy, and are happy to delegate this to true representatives — but so that they may, if necessary, discipline an unresponsive government. For this purpose, we need *recall*, so that incompetent politicians can be fired midterm if sufficient numbers of their constituents are unhappy; referendums, so that the people may, if they wish, give the final assent to any nation-changing legislation; and citizen-initiatives, a process by which the people may create a new law directly, if needed, and force a parliament that has resisted the people to pass that law.

In times past, when central governments restricted themselves to remote national and international concerns, and constitutionally to rules, not deals, such tools were less needed and the idea of political "representatives" made sense. Today, however, when central governments all over the world are increasingly interventionist, gobbling up half and more of the people's resources and attempting to regulate family life, local moral standards, abortion, educational materials, religion, and so on, the people rightly complain: "Enough! Now we must have control!" They will get it by these means.

13. A Fiscal Guillotine and Tax Limitation

Political leaders are presently unaccountable. They regularly plunge their constituents into unconscionable debt, and then, instead of going to jail, walk away on a handsome pension for life.

So there must be *tax limitation clause* in our national constitution — and in every provincial constitution — to prevent the legal plunder of the people's resources. After all, your hard-earned wealth is your private property, but it means very little if the State takes most of it away. Tax Freedom Day in Canada as of 1994 is somewhere around July 7 of each year. This means we work more than half the year for government. We are tax slaves for half our working lives.

A simple tax limitation clause would constitutionally restrict each province to a fixed percentage of Gross Provincial Product (say fifteen percent), which the people, by referendum, or an incoming party by popular mandate, could raise or lower at will.[29] Any deficit financing through borrowing would be included in the percentage, thus blocking escape from the powers of the clause. One problem would then be the federal government's downloading of its own shortfalls onto provincial governments. So the whole system has to change. An answer to the shortfall/dumping problem would be to forbid any direct taxation of the people by the federal government. Instead, let the provinces agree on what percentage of their Gross Provincial Product they should fork over each year to Ottawa for its restricted national duties.

Another powerful remedy for deficit spending would be a rule such as the following: "Any government that incurs a deficit two years in a row may be put to an election at the option of the people." That will have them minding their pennies.

14. *The Four F's*

Canada is a nation culturally and historically based on Freedom, Family, Free Enterprise, and Faith: on the importance of the exercise of personal freedom and responsibility by each citizen (as opposed to life by State dictate, or the General Will); on the recognition and protection of the natural family — a married mother and father living together with their dependent children (not as our only, but certainly as our most important social institution); on the right of individuals and families to voluntary economic exchange (as opposed to a growing State control, taxation, and regulation of the economy); and finally, on the important role of faith in a free society, whereby individuals may choose to shape their lives by moral values higher than those promoted by the State (and thereby thwart the State's efforts to control their values). The Four F's, and everything they imply, are the true unwritten, living constitution of a free society.

IV

THE DYNAMICS OF DECLINE

How a Constitution, Meant to Preserve Society, Can Destroy It

---

The simplest way to understand how this Charter-assisted process of social decay works is to understand that all nations are internally divided into three levels with respect to how they control themselves, as follows:

- *The State*, which relies on *formal*, involuntary control (laws, coercion, police)
- *Civil Society*, which relies on *informal*, voluntary control (parents, employers, clergy, officers of organizations, etc.)
- *Individuals*, who rely on *personal* control (self-restraint)

The uppermost level in all nations is the State itself, or the apparatus of government. It is coercive by nature, enjoying a legal monopoly on power, such that our only meaningful political freedom is to change our master from time to time. Plainly, this form of authority is formal and involuntary, in the sense that individuals cannot directly affect it. Without any checks and balances, this level of authority would eventually and naturally spread to control everyone and everything. In a modern liberal society, however, in which power is gained and the thirst for more satisfied by votes, not guns, the democratic State, to ensure its hold on power, must deliver, or be seen to deliver, the goods to all citizens equally, regardless of their wealth or station in life. Such states grow in power and decline in freedom because their ostensible dedication to the public good as dictated by their egalitarian philosophy obligates them to make larger and ever more widespread and expensive promises in exchange for votes. So to be seen as just, and because they are forced by the logic of modern liberalism to argue that none may be excluded, such states inevitably generate written constitutions — a kind of promissory note — the better to control their millions of restless individuals, buying their support and loyalty with promises of material equality (the costs of which are habitually financed by future generations of the unborn). Because tyrannical power is not a viable democratic option, every effort of government must be directed towards the cultivation of loyalty to the State and its values, and all competition for that loyalty must be diminished, if not eliminated.

So a simple strategy develops for producing loyalty by marketing the State and its programs to the people (whether they like it or not), and once enshrined in written law, quickly engenders *an egalitarian commitment to end all privileges* (other than those of the rulers), however minute, wherever found, suspected, perceived, alleged, whether real or imaginary. And paradoxically, the more equal the citizens do become in reality, the more intensely are their minute continuing differences felt — and therefore the more intensely must these be eradicated.

At the bottom of this structure is a huge mass of individuals, each walking around with the approved set of enumerated rights and freedoms in his or her head, wondering "What's in it for me?"

But we must be clear: a mass of individuals is not a society. It has no concentrated purpose, form, or being. It's just a mob. Each person is an autonomous individual, or, as I like to put it, a purpose looking for a cause. The State at the top? Millions of aimless individuals at the bottom? So where is what we call "society"?

Well, there's the rub.

The middle, or intermediate, level of social reality is quite different from the top and bottom levels, and constitutes civil society itself. Its dominant characteristic is that it is made up of millions of voluntary groups to which most of those autonomous individuals may either belong, or strive to belong. Here is where we find the many millions of families, corporations, charitable organizations, sports teams, clubs, academic groups, scientific groups, children's organizations, arts groups, self-help groups, and so on, each made vital and dynamic by virtue of its inherent purposes, relationships, loyalties, and activities.

The English term for these groups is "voluntary associations," or "intermediate associations." The French term is *corps intermédiaire*. These terms imply that civil society is somehow secondary, or sandwiched between, or dependent upon individuals and the State for its existence. Whereas I argue that the primary reality of all human existence is civil society itself, which in turn gives birth to new individuals, who must be nourished and raised up to take their place in that society, and that the State, a creation of civil society, must answer to society, and not vice versa.

THE FOUR FEATURES OF A CIVIL SOCIETY

Civil societies are a complex matrix of millions of these voluntary, interacting groups, all of which have four basic characteristics not found at the other two levels. These four characteristics are profoundly emblematic of all human social life, and just as profoundly anti-egalitarian. This creates the serious dilemma of an anti-egalitarian society within an egalitarian State, and sets these two against each other in a kind of battle to the death for predominance. Or rather, a battle to decay, since society is by far the more compelling, but also by far the weaker of the two. The simple process I am about to describe has occurred in every civilization in history, explains much about the fall of civilizations, and is actively at work in our midst.

What are the four characteristics? In order to enter any voluntary association of human beings, whether we are speaking of the Boy Scouts, a marriage, or membership in a club, there will always be found a kind of solemn right of passage, whether simple or complex, the characteristics of which are sacrifice, subordination, commitment, and privilege.

Sacrifice refers to the requirement of all social groups that individuals aspiring to join must voluntarily agree to place the common will of the group above their own personal needs. They must aspire to the internal values and emotional bonds of the group. From this flows loyalty. The motto of common organizations like Rotary International, for example, is "Service Above Self." If this willingness to sacrifice for others is reversed, if any member puts himself above the group, he will usually be forced out.

Subordination refers to the requirement that all members must submit to the authority and rules of the group. This is a requirement for group discipline. Insubordination normally triggers some internal process for dismissing, disowning, or firing, and all members carry around an internal understanding of the rules by which they feel bound and are proudly distinguished from non-members. Members get expelled, Boy Scouts get demoted, spouses get divorced.

Commitment is the process whereby, the first two requirements having been met, a member is asked formally to make a vow, or public commitment, to the group. Boy Scouts, marriage partners, and club members make their commitment in words, written contract, or deed, to the ideals and activities they share. An important point here is that any autonomous individuals who choose not to go through this process will never be coerced to do so — membership is entirely voluntary — but neither will they get to the last stage. In fact, they will be *visibly and intentionally excluded* from it.

Privilege is the last stage whereby the group approves the bestowal of specific benefits and protections on each qualified member. This is often accompanied by a significant ceremony in which the commitment or vow of loyalty is made, and by special symbols or costume intended to distinguish members from non-members. Boy Scouts get to wear their caps and kerchiefs, and say secret things; marital partners sign covenants, wear rings, get lawful and exclusive access to each other, and in a procreative society become eligible for certain legal, tax, and social privileges historically not available to the unmarried. Signed-up club members are expected to be loyal, carry cards, be dutiful, pay their dues, do required club work, abide by rules, and so on.

By now you can see what I'm getting at.

All social groups are defined by their eagerness to *distinguish* not in a negative but in a very positive sense, between members and non-members. In fact all of civil society, you might say, is a vast organism that hovers over the great undifferentiated mass of autonomous individuals, seeking to lure them into making sacrifices and commitments to its own far more challenging and difficult life. By this four-step process, society seeks not only to *select*, but to *direct*. As long as individuals demonstrate a clear willingness to graduate from individual autonomy to social interdependence, then through its preferential treatment, society breathes the warmth of human community into their souls. Then, and only then, will society confer its positive benefits, status, and protection on those who voluntarily opt into its preferred social forms. Importantly, however, it has no wish to harm those who refuse to opt in. It merely waits for them. Their freedoms and rights as autonomous individuals, meanwhile, remain intact. They will not get less than the common rights and freedoms of all individuals. But, until very recently, they certainly could not get more unless they opted into this social process. *It is a process inherently preferential, and exclusionary, and the modern radical project is to circumvent, even to destroy, this process.*

In deadly contrast to civil society, however, the interventionist egalitarian State is defined by its almost evangelical eagerness to *equalize* everyone.

So what we have here is a recipe for deadly conflict between the dynamics of the living society itself and the aims of the power-hungry State (every State, by degrees). Now we know why in the process of creating its various constitutions, the State seldom protects or promotes society (the common law does that), but rather protects and promotes only the autonomous individual. For the State seeks actively to diminish the multifarious voluntary social loyalties individuals naturally seek — to get rid of the competition — and graft these loyalties onto itself.[30] In other words, the State seeks to convert the *social* membership in voluntary groups into a *political* relationship between individuals and the State. It wants no differences, no rites of passage, no membership, no privileges, and no exclusions other than those approved, conferred, or provided by the State itself (Rousseau would be happy).

The heart of the State's explicit and implicit strategy for increasing allegiance to itself is to offer and supply tax-funded services, protections, and benefits equally to all individuals, thus undercutting the drawing power of social groups that normally provide for each other, and that also normally exclude non-conforming individuals. In this way, the State successfully diminishes or eliminates entirely the positive distinctions and allegiances normal to the very life of such groups. In other words, the State steals its customers from the living society, hoping for a dead society and a living State — a moral contradiction, for society is based on voluntary authority (morally alive), and the State on involuntary authority (morally dead).

Thus do democratic states that have allowed themselves to be transformed into modern egalitarian ones consume their own societies in a suicidal civil war of values that pitches individual rights against society's rights.

This process of social breakdown is particularly well advanced in North America, where a huge variety of codes and charters created by every conceivable level of government is being used aggressively by interest groups to claim egalitarian individual rights. Whether for family, tax, or legal privileges and immunities, spousal benefits, private property rights of landlords or owners, or commercial rights of enterprises, or access to formerly private clubs — it matters not. Wherever enough angry individuals can be found who want the social benefits, privileges, and protections of a particular social group or class, *without having to pay the stipulated price* of personal sacrifice, subordination, or commitment, they will use egalitarian codes and charters to argue that they are "discriminated" against because they are excluded from some status, benefit, or privilege — and therefore the State is not fulfilling its egalitarian mandate. This brings the power of the State to bear mightily against all civil society.

In essence, the modern notion of charter "rights" is being used successfully as a battering ram to attack those ancient rights of society that are constitutive of civil society itself, and have long been recognized in the common law — *but not in charter law*. This means that in a contest between the two forms of law, some unelected judge will call the shots. If he is a modern liberal, he will rule in favour of egalitarian individual rights and against society's rights. And it is interesting that, as Felix Morley put it, in the British-derived nations, the common law (and the U.S. Constitution) make a clear distinction between society and State. But "Rousseau's refusal to make any such distinction has been widely accepted in Europe, and is indeed a tenet of European socialistic as well as communistic thought."[31] Ditto for Canadian socialists, and our Charter, which makes no such distinction. So it is time to tremble as a people, for whenever individuals successfully use charters to obtain such benefits without earning them, society is in big trouble. They are not merely changing society; they are bleeding it to death.

So we try in vain to imagine a world in which little boys — or girls — demand the right to wear Boy Scout uniforms without qualifying for them; where young men and women and homosexuals demand the legal, tax, and even commercial advantages and privileges of married couples, without submitting to the difficult procreative sexual order of society (on which even their own existence depends); where non-members claim the rights and benefits of groups for which they have not qualified; where the sanctity of privacy and the rights of private and commercial property are brought down; and where the natural propensity of all human beings to create meaningful positive social distinctions and privileges is driven underground.

Modern written charters and constitutions, with their entrenched egalitarianism, positive rights, and imperative and arbitrary law, are now the *central weapon* in this radical war against all natural social distinction and privilege. When there is no meaningful society left, when it is sufficiently weakened, slack, and torpid, when there is intolerable crime in the streets and the schools, when drugs and disease mount their eager claims, when every window in every home is barred, when political and social cynicism reign supreme, there will be only one "family" to consider: the all-controlling State, cultivating allegiance, even grateful admiration and obedience from its millions of autonomous and utterly dependent children, even as it expires.

We have brought this upon ourselves in the name of rights and freedoms.

V

THE CRACK-UP

The Coming Showdown
With Quebec

On **October 25, 1993**, as final results of Canada's federal election poured in, a new political map of Canada materialized simultaneously on millions of television screens, and threw the future of one of the world's most noble democracies into stark relief. As if suddenly freed from a confusion of constitutional bandages, our national linguistic and cultural tensions appeared on stage personified, before a quizzical populace. Suddenly, the problem of Quebec was front and centre.

We have already seen how charter law can displace the concept of inherent freedom and the common law, two cornerstones of a free society, and how this egalitarian effect can

90

radically diminish, even destroy, much of natural civil society. Let us now explore briefly how the general concepts entrenched in Canada's Charter have produced a predictable reaction from Quebec, and thereby threatened Confederation itself. For although Quebec nationalism has always been present in Canada, the strength of the recent French-Canadian desire for separation must be understood in large part as a reaction to Canada's Charter-imposed, interventionist welfare State regime, without which Quebec disgruntlement would be an ongoing but minor irritant on the body politic. In short, the Charter, an instrument by which Trudeau meant to quell or at least diffuse Quebec nationalism, has ended by actually stimulating it.

But the great sleep continues.

This is a wake-up call.

How are we going to deal with a province of Canada that refuses to fly Canada's flag and calls its provincial legislature a "National Assembly," and its premier "Prime Minister"?

I suggest that if as a nation we wish to escape strife and bloodshed in the near future, if we wish to avoid the fate of Ireland, Yugoslavia, and other divided nations that have devoured themselves over lines on the map, then we have at the very least a duty to ask the right questions. Then, if any of us end up patriotic Canadians abandoned in Quebec, or if we suddenly discover our shipments to eastern customers cannot pass through Quebec, or if our sons are called upon to defend Canadian citizens or a federal airport inside Quebec, we will not be able to say we never dreamed it could happen.

THE BIG LIE WAS JUST THE BEGINNING

Canadians have been spoon-fed an official big lie by their own governments ever since the mid-1960s. The big lie says that "the Canadian nation was created by two founding peoples," the English and the French, and that Canada is "an equal partnership between two founding races."

Nothing could be further from the truth. The nation of Canada, as we saw earlier, did not exist as a federal nation until 1867 when the existing provinces under the British Crown created the federal nation of Canada, not as two people, but as a single people in four provinces. The parts created the whole, not the other way around, and race, culture, and language had nothing to do with it. (It was only after this initial "creation of the nation," so to speak, that the nation in turn created, or *enlarged*, provinces, such as Quebec, *as provinces of Canada*.)

As the distinguished Canadian historian Donald Creighton put it in his article "The Myth of Biculturalism or the Great French-Canadian Sales Campaign" (*Saturday Night*, September 1966), no one at any of the three conferences called to create Confederation, at Charlottetown, Quebec, or London, "would have dreamed . . . of constituting such a meeting along ethnic or cultural lines." And further, "there was nothing that remotely approached a general declaration of principle that Canada was to be a bilingual or bicultural nation." The late Senator Eugene Forsey, another constitutional expert, insisted that "over and over again, the 'Canadian' Fathers of Confederation, French,

English, Irish, Scotch, declared emphatically that they were creating a new nation . . . ." In fact, frightened by French continental despotism and the American civil war, French Canadians in particular welcomed the stability of English rule. Sir George Etienne Cartier himself declared in public debate that if union could be obtained, Canadians "would form a political nationality with which neither the national origin, nor the religion of any individual, would interfere." Sir Hector-Louis Langevin, a Father of Confederation, declared proudly in 1865 that "in [the new] Parliament there will be no question of race, nationality, religion or locality . . ."[32]

So when the Quebec legislature was completed in 1883, they carved into its Coat of Arms the words "Je Me Souviens," today inscribed on Quebec licence plates and taken to imply a longing for former French rule. Ironically, these words were taken from a short verse composed by Eugène Taché, architect of the Quebec legislature building and Deputy Minister of Public Works. The full verse read:

Je me souviens
Que né sous le lys
Je fleuris sous la rose.

This translates as a verse commemorating the peaceful blending of peoples in early Canada:

I remember
That born under the [French] lily
I flourish under the [English] rose.

That was a great vision. But in 1963, less than a hundred years later, on the cusp of the centralizing welfare State that he initiated, Liberal prime minister Lester B. Pearson created the Royal Commission on Bilingualism and Biculturalism, and in it basically directed all commissioners to find ways to build Canada not as a *single* people, but as an *equal bi-racial partnership* between *two* founding peoples — despite their huge numerical difference.

This was the linchpin of the Liberal government's strategy to centralize and unify Canada's coming welfare State, in this case through an enforced linguistic and cultural policy meant to please and pacify a noisy separatist minority in a province without whose votes no party could win a federal election by giving them a status equal to that of the English, from sea to sea. In fact, without the Quebec bloc vote he needed, Canadians would have returned a Conservative government.

Pearson's government specifically directed the commissioners *to change the basic character of this single nation* and establish it as a union of *two* equal, racially defined nations. Not long afterward, a federal minister named Jean-Luc Pepin spoke often of himself, Trudeau, Pelletier, Marchand, Lalonde — and Jean Chrétien — as "a well-organized group of revolutionaries" who fully intended to achieve this radical equalization. On November 13, 1982, fourteen years after Pierre Trudeau first became Prime Minister of Canada, his Secretary of State, Serge Joyal, made a public speech to the Fedération acadienne de la Nouvelle-Ecosse. He spoke euphorically of "making Canada a French country both inside and outside Quebec," adding that in Canada's Charter could be found "the real foundation of French" and the strategy to change Canada. He said that it was hard "for some of our fellow Canadians who speak the other language to accept the fact that Canada is a French state."[33]

A CLASH OF CENTRALISMS

But this strategy was doomed from the start for two simple reasons. First, it never had the consent of the people of Canada. It lacked legitimacy. And second, the main pressure felt by the French minority confined within Quebec, a minority historically partial to the centralizing mentality, was the imposition on it of the much larger and even more centralizing and interventionist Canadian welfare State, especially as geared up by Canada's father of socialism, Prime Minister Trudeau, a man Quebec nationalists came to hate. In other words — and it seems that English Canada has not yet understood this — the essence not of French-Canadian discontent (which will always be with us), but of the growing populist appeal of separation, was *the clash between two centralizing forces within one nation*, neither one of which could succeed if the other did.

But this is very well understood by the separatist leader Jacques Parizeau, and by Lucien Bouchard, leader of the Bloc Québécois. Both know that there is no reconciliation possible between two competing forces striving for centralized control of different pieces of the same soil; between two competing visions of a common French-style, top-down collectivist nation, the one

Quebec nationalist, the other Canadian nationalist (and internationalist). As Trudeau remarked in 1991, "I am amused to say that Mr. Parizeau, the leader of the Parti Québécois, is constantly quoted as agreeing with me and he's told me that to my face, too. He says: 'You know, you and I agree on everything, that there has to be a strong central government, except I want its capital to be in Quebec City and you want it to be in Ottawa.' "[34]

So the reality here is that of a more or less homogeneous Quebec, naturally determined to preserve and strengthen her French culture and top-down controls, within a larger State with a top-down agenda of its own. What we have is a small circle inside a very large one. Two French-style mentalities at war on the same turf. As Quebec columnist William Johnson put it, French Canadians, after generations of blaming themselves for their failings, have rediscovered their historical scapegoat. The new intellectual orthodoxy in Quebec says that "the essential state of alienation of Quebecers is because there is a federal government and two official languages, and because of the colonizers, *les anglais*."[35]

It is also true that during the 1960s and afterward there was a serious international threat to Canadian federation posed by the efforts of France, a country that was eager when led by Charles de Gaulle to strengthen the failing French presence in the world. As York University professor J. L. Granatstein has pointed out, in the 1960s and thereafter France gave large sums of money, sent some three thousand military conscripts here to work as secret agents, teachers, and revolutionaries, and gave many other forms of "assistance" which were meant, as an angry Trudeau put it, "to demolish the unity of Canada."[36] Granatstein described France's spy efforts here as "a declaration of war on Canada's continued national existence."

So the combination of three realities — the presence of a large minority of French-Canadian voters who had to be kept happy, external interference from France, and the Liberal government's persistent vision of a burgeoning welfare State — meant that the only solution (for a committed socialist) was *to make the whole of Canada more socialist and more French* in style. Here was a small group of elite men deciding what the General Will ought to be, and damn well forcing Canada into their mould. This "solution" was also supported by most academic observers, simply because most of them are fellow-travellers with the socialist mentality.

Hardly anyone suggested that Quebec, like the other provinces, might have fought much harder to defend its place within Canada if our federal system had not been twisted out of shape; if all the provinces been left alone with their precious freedoms to be themselves — sovereign provinces in a sovereign nation — rather than pushed into a larger, homogenizing welfare State. If we had followed Locke, instead of Rousseau. For surely it is a love of freedom and privacy under common laws and principles that unites a people, not common government social programs and subsidies. The latter is a recipe for a nation of morally anesthetized beggars united only by their common envy. It is a recipe for turning Canada into a holding tank for losers.

But our anxious utopians were caught in a trap formed by their own thinking: it was contrary to the evolving logic of modern liberalism to reverse the welfare State, so they had to create the big lie. This meant there would have to be a struggle to the death between two top-down mentalities on the same turf. The Charter, with its imposed and entrenched bilingualism and redistributive schemes, would be the essential federal instrument for the implementation of this master plan throughout Canada, the coercive language-engineering provisions of which alone have cost Canadians about $25 billion since inception. It would initiate what columnist Richard Gwyn described as "nothing less than a social revolution." In fact, it may have cost us Confederation, because there was bound to be a reaction to such an unnatural program. In fact, after his $25-million report to the government on the mood of Canadians in 1992, Keith Spicer — one of the architects of official bilingualism, and a former Official Languages Commissioner — said that "the extent of consensus against official language policy is remarkable. [Official bilingualism is rejected] almost universally" (*Toronto Sun*, March 22, 1992).

The predictable result was that by 1993 Canada had two large minority parties in Parliament, each determined to end the big lie — one, the Bloc Québécois, wishing to separate from Confederation altogether; the other, the Reform Party of Canada, wishing to refederalize the nation on equal terms for all provinces: to return to the original meaning of federalism, or else negotiate the separation of Quebec. Here were two elected political symbols of the clash between the French and English styles.

So the stage is set, and in order to prepare ourselves for what is in effect the fallout of our own Constitution, surely we should be asking, What is the truth about so-called separation? Is it legal? Who owns what? Who's calling the shots? What will happen to Canada? What is a confederation, anyway?

A CONFEDERATION IS LIKE A CO-OP

Try to imagine that you and nine of your friends (together making the ten provinces) have all seen a building you wish to purchase that is suitable for ten apartments. Together, you enter into an agreement to purchase it based on equal ownership. It's a co-op. By written agreement, each of you gets a certain amount of living space, some of the benefits, and some of the costs, depending on the size of your family, but nothing prevents anyone from relocating within the building, by mutual agreement, and nothing prevents you as a group from agreeing to reshape the interior. You all own the whole building equally.

One day, nine of you arrive home from work to find François, chain saw in hand, attempting to cut his apartment away from the building. He is angry. Nobody loves him. He says he wants to leave and "take what I own." Imagine the justifiable and spontaneous outrage from the rest:

"We all own this building together. You have no right to reconfigure the building without our permission. We all got into this deal together, and no one can change it without unanimous consent. Anyway, you owe us a lot of money. We subsidized you from the start. Even if we decide that we will let you out of this deal, you will have to settle up with us for what you owe, and maybe even pay damages for devaluing our building."

So there it is. A confederation of provinces is like a co-op apartment building. All Canadian citizens, regardless of where they live for the moment, own Canada equally. The lines on the map for each province (like each apartment wall) are there for administrative and political convenience but do not confer ownership of real assets on the citizens of any province. When French Canadians (we cannot say "Québécois," because many who live in Quebec are quite happy to remain Canadians) attempt to saw off Quebec and cart it away, they are trying to take it away from all of us without permission. They are breaking their contract.

Based on this understanding, I suggest there are three huge issues around which any dialogue must eventually revolve. They are the issues of permission, partition, and duplication.

PERMISSION — OR, WHO SAYS YOU CAN LEAVE?

Is separation legal? Can a province just walk away from Confederation? Does any province have the legal right to leave? The answer is a flat "no."

Senator Eugene Forsey stated repeatedly in his last years that *no province of Canada has the right to leave Confederation without the unanimous approval of all the other provinces.* This is easily verifiable by other legal experts. As Canadian historian Kenneth McNaught has written, Canadian provinces have "no constitutional right of secession," and "legally, constitutionally, the provinces of Canada have no independent legitimacy." This means that no province of Canada, having entered Confederation, has any rights outside the Constitution. Any attempt to break away would be tantamount to revolution.

Consent from all was required to join Confederation by signing the BNA Act of 1867 — an agreement to which Quebec was party. Logically and legally, consent from all is a prerequisite to changing Confederation. Any international court would likely agree.

What this means is that if any province of Canada wishes to separate, it must have the consent of Canada's House of Commons, and a majority, if not all, of the provincial legislatures. In other words, our national dialogue on separation is upside down. Everyone is talking about Quebec holding a referendum on separation, as if Quebec alone can decide the fate of this nation. But the reality is exactly the opposite. Canada as a whole must deliberate the underlying terms and principles of separation and then, if desired, hold a national refrendum to determine whether separation can be allowed or, indeed, whether expulsion might be preferable. In short, any such permission must be on terms and conditions that satisfy not only the province seceding, but also all the other provinces from whom it is attempting to secede. As constitutional lawyer Stephen Scott of McGill University has written, "It seems preposterous to assert that Canada can be brought to an end at any time at the demand of one of its provinces."[37]

What If They Try to Go It Alone?

But what if Quebec says, "To hell with your permission, I'm getting out!" and starts up the chain saw again? Well, that's what's called a Unilateral Declaration of Independence. A UDI, a form of "self-determination," elicits a certain amount of sympathy from freedom lovers around the world who like to see countries free themselves from oppression. By declaring a UDI, French Canadians would be appealing not to other Canadians, whom they would spite by such a tactic, but to the international community. After all, in the long run its is the international community that confers sovereignty on a nation through official recognition. If no one recognizes your declaration of independence, you haven't got a separate country. But let us pause here.

Arguably, far from being oppressed, Quebec is one of the freest territories in the world. It has also been massively subsidized by Canada for a very long time — according to University of Calgary economist Robert Mansell, Quebec received $160 billion from 1961 to 1991 and has enjoyed a standard of living higher than if it had been left on its own. Much higher. The argument that Quebec is oppressed, or has become oppressed over time, and thus has some democratic right to secede, would not stand up in our own Supreme Court or in any international courts of law. A UDI would break our own law, and likely the international law of equity.

An even more dangerous reality is that while for any referendum on separation Quebec nationalists would surely insist that a simple majority of fifty-one percent means victory, many experts would argue that for a matter so serious, a "special majority" of two-thirds, or even seventy-five percent, ought to be required. After all, a mere simple majority basis would mean that fully one half of all the citizens of Quebec — up to 3.4 million Canadian citizens (!) —

who have paid taxes and given allegiance to Canada all their lives and who clearly prefer to live in their own ancestral homes as Canadian citizens, would be forced either to live in a separate country, or emigrate. What about their livelihoods, citizenship, passports, property, investments, rights to education, and so on? In effect, they would be the "minority" on whose rights separatists would trample in principle, and with delight. Here we have a living example of why a "pure democracy" can be a bad idea. This situation illustrates with force why the founders of Canada and America feared unfettered democracy as a form of legalized mob rule.

As we might expect, Canadian citizens left behind in Quebec would scream for protection, and Ottawa would be morally and legally bound to help them. After all, North America has had one disastrous example of this dilemma already, during the U.S. civil war when a minority of southerners attempted to secede from the union. There were lots of Americans in the south who wanted to stay American. And then as now, American states, like Canadian provinces, had no right to secede. Lincoln, McNaught explains, "believed that in a federal union there is no legal-constitutional right of unrestricted self-determination," and he clearly recognized the obligation of any federal government to protect the property and liberties of individual citizens entrapped in such a situation, as well as to defend federal property.[38]

For Canada, the same dilemma draws the same conclusions. The Parliament of Canada is legally bound to defend and protect the territorial integrity of the nation against all invaders or enemies, within or without our borders, and any force used to dismember

Canada constitutes a treasonous and criminal action. So by this same reasoning, and very likely the same rationalizations, we can expect federal intervention and force. We could get civil war.

By now, the idea of a UDI ought to be looking awfully messy. And let us remember that Canada's traditional response to instability is swift and violent. Canadian authorities, in the defence of "Peace, Order, and good Government," have engaged in all sorts of wars, massacres, petty rebellions, supressions of union strikes, Indian violence, mining violence, and the like. Canada even has a rather colourful history of pre-emptive force in the "apprehension" of violence. The federal army was readily deployed at Montreal, in 1970, and at Oka, in 1990 (both times at the request of the premier of an ostensibly separatist province). We can be fairly sure the army will be used elsewhere, if necessary.[39] From our own history, at least, we cannot predict a peaceful handling of such a crisis.

PARTITION — OR WHAT CAME IN, GOES OUT

Well here's another problem. As I said, the lines on the map, like the partitions inside the building, are just there by common agreement for administrative and political convenience. The lines do not bestow a right of ownership or sovereignty on anyone. If on Monday you move to Quebec you cannot say on that first day that you own part of Quebec. Just as, if you move back to Ontario on Tuesday, you cannot then say you own part of Ontario and have surrendered whatever it was you owned of the province of Quebec on Monday. Just try to imagine the "ownership" of each province switching around every time hundreds of thousands of Canadians decide to migrate internally each year. Anyway, figure it out. Who, other than the people themselves, could possibly own Canada? Their governments, right? But democratic governments represent the people as a whole. And governments come and go. So we are left with the people as owners of the whole. And make no mistake. The taxes you pay every year on Canada's federal debt are not earmarked by province. You're paying off debt for the whole nation. It's your debt. Your nation. So even if Quebec gets nasty and tries to declare a UDI, the battle will quickly shift from lines on the map to arguments over what *property* French Canadians actually own and want to take out of Confederation as real assets.

This takes us straight into treaty law to find out what portions of the province were actually ceded or transferred to Quebec; the real question, in other words, is not about *separation*, but about *partition*, a distinction most of us have heard nothing about. But our various governments know this distinction very well, and they consider the whole topic too volatile for our poor little heads. And the media are rather silent on the whole matter.

There are many books and articles on the subject of what it is that French Canadians actually own.[40] Here's what it boils down to: Quebec came into Confederation as a much smaller province than it is now. About two-thirds of that province — a vast cornucopia of future extractable wealth — used to be called Rupert's Land and was ceded by Britain to Canada, then by Canada to

Quebec in two parcels in 1898 and 1912, to be administered by Quebec *as a province of Canada*, not by Quebec as a separate nation. In effect, Rupert's Land was given to Canada, then transferred to Quebec under the Crown, in trusteeship. And as Newfoundland's Premier Clyde Wells put it, "The Canadian people would not have added to Quebec if there had been any prospect that it would cease to be part of Canada." Strictly speaking, if Quebec attempts to separate, the added land should by legal right transfer back to Britain! Now that's bizarre. Such a result could be legally avoided only if Quebec seceded peaceably as an independent monarchy, enabling it to retain those lands. Try to imagine His Majesty, King Parizeau.

But the underlying argument over partition is that if French Canadians wish to leave, they should be allowed to take out of Confederation only what they brought into it in 1867, minus their share of our national debt. You can see the problem, because when push comes to shove, the French-Canadian "people" (make no mistake, this is not a conflict over territory, but over culture and race) could only lay a bona-fide legal treaty claim to an oblong strip of land running from west of Montreal, north about a hundred miles, then east to Labrador, and paralleled by a coastal strip on the south side of the St. Lawrence River. Other "peoples" have settled the rest of Quebec.

Then there is the St. Lawrence Seaway, which is controlled internationally, not by Canada alone, and must remain international. Certainly Canada will demand the free passage of ships. And there are large groups of French Canadians living in Ontario along the border of Quebec, and in New Brunswick, whom Quebec would want to annex. And there is the problem of land and air defence and security, and Canada's treaty obligations with NATO over Quebec airspace. There would have to be a renegotiation of the free trade deal; there would be an instant flight of capital. And what about the problem of Quebec owing Canada $125 billion or more (twenty-four percent of our $500-billion federal debt, as of January 1994, one that is climbing at $86,000 per minute)? Oh, and citizen Raymond Aaron has already filed a class-action suit (November 1992) on behalf of all Canadian voters, claiming $500 billion in damages because the Bloc Québécois is bringing down property values and incomes with its campaign for separation (*Globe and Mail*, January 24, 1994). And there is the Trojan Horse problem that most of Canada's key federal ministries and departments are heavily staffed by francophones — some to the sixty-percent level, or higher. Do we think they are going to argue for Canada?

Given this volatile mixture, we can be fairly certain that somewhere in the Pentagon there is a small room devoted to the military analysis of this situation. And . . . as international peacekeeper, it would not be difficult for America, with "a well-equipped and powerful light division based at Fort Drum, N.Y., one that is trained in cold-weather operations, [and] a major air base at Plattsburgh, N.Y.," to justify a brief military peacekeeping invasion to protect its Canadian assets and to stop the bloodshed — in the name of international stability — right?[41]

DUPLICATION — WHAT'S GOOD FOR THE GOOSE, IS GOOD FOR THE GANDER

The opening gambit of Quebec nationalists is to avoid the topic of partition altogether, hoping to uphold a claim to all Quebec territory on the present map. They even lay claim to all of Labrador, which has been controlled by Newfoundland since 1927! But this is only a bargaining chip. Once at the table, they will likely start by magnanimously agreeing to give up their claim to Labrador — if Canada will give them everything else. Canada will then insist on enclaves and a corridor to protect Canadian citizens there. Quebec will refuse. Canada will then refuse to grant Quebec a Hydro corridor to sell its power, and will threaten to suspend the close to $4 billion in annual transfer payments Quebec now receives from Canada (which would cease at separation, anyway). Well, anyone can see how the sparks are going to fly.

But let us suppose that somehow Quebec succeeds with the argument of self-determination. Why, then, should that same argument not be duplicated for the many enclaves of English Canadians, and other non-French minorities? Why should they not use the same arguments to separate from the newly partitioned Quebec? Surely separatists cannot argue that Canada is divisible but Quebec is not. They reply that these other minority groups are not a "people," or that in the case of the English minority, they already have a "people" outside Quebec, in Canada proper. Now that's a stretcher. Just think of some densely populated enclaves within Quebec such as West Montreal with its more than 400,000 English-speaking people. There is already a serious bid from "Quebec West" as a new province carved from Quebec, comprised of about one million people. At the least, such groups will demand to be partitioned out of Quebec as a Canadian enclave, and will want travel corridors, as mentioned already. That's what West Berliners had in East Germany. With so many enclaves that would surely vote to stay in Canada, the new Quebec "nation" would look like a piece of Swiss cheese. By now, François' chain saw has stopped, and all the noses are bloodied.

And how about Canada's native and Inuit people? They are obviously a "people" in any sense of the term. In fact, in addition to language and culture they also have a racial distinctiveness, which is not the case for all francophones. And they have themselves already laid serious treaty land claims to more than seventy-five percent of the province of Quebec (and most other provinces). So we can be assured that all native peoples currently under the jurisdiction of Ottawa and enjoying its considerable largesse (about $15,000 per capita annually) will want to continue this way, especially as French Canadians have a history of cultural disdain for native peoples.

It is time for a full national dialogue.

VI

RECONSTITUTION

Becoming Whole Again

Just as the normal tensions of the French-Canadian minority within Confederation were grossly exacerbated by the rise of the controlling welfare State, the solution, if we wish to keep Quebec in Confederation, is to relieve the tensions by reversing this process. Canada must once again put her noble roots down deep into true federalism: a sovereign nation of sovereign provinces, with powers strictly divided. Such a true federal structure protects democracy, without which, we get what we have seen — increasingly heavy-handed and expensive centralism. We must scrap our welfare-State Charter. Return to our common-law roots. Reinstate and entrench the sovereignty of Parliament. Ensure that the lawmakers of last resort are the people, not the courts, which must be restricted to adjudication of the laws and division of powers. In short, big central government, along with with the Charter that helped make it so officially prevalent, must withdraw from all provinces at once. The State must surrender any right to legally define or control the people's freedoms. Then we must trash the morally illegitimate and fiscally irresponsible redistributive programs of the welfare State, pay off the public debt, then slash taxes and leave the people free to control their own resources.

It can be done. Switzerland has a standard of living as high or higher than our own, for half the cost in total taxes as a percentage of GDP. We must speak only of freedoms protected equally by the law, not of rights, or outcomes. Then Quebec, like every other province, could live in peace and tolerably run its own affairs. Canada as a whole must travel from its current status as a top-down State, back to a free, bottom-up society, or Quebec will be lost, and Confederation, too. This is the only solution consistent with our historical vision of a free federation of peoples that will keep Canada as we know it together, a people bound not by any common envy for equal outcomes, but by a fierce love of common principles and a just law.

After this refederalization, when all provinces are once again distinct, more sovereign, and unencumbered by intrusive federal welfare-State coercion, subsidies, and controls, what would Quebec do? She would do what comes naturally to the French. She would continue to run her own provincial welfare State. That is the French way. And as long as the whole nation is radically decentralized, this can be easily accommodated within

Confederation. And they can pay for it themselves. That is the beauty of the federal solution. It establishes a context in which governments at all levels must compete to please the local tax-payer. Then other Canadians would not be dragged along by the centralizing mentality to please Quebec, or any other province, either fiscally, or politically, as they have been since the 1960s.

One thing, at least, is certain. We must either recognize the huge mistake of imposed, Charter-dictated egalitarianism, and its ruinous effect on Confederation — of which Quebec is but the most visible political and cultural manifestation — or learn the hard way. Either we admit the mistake, and hasten to return to our root values and principles: freedom, not forced equality; family, not the welfare State; free enterprise, not central planning and regulation; confidence in moral values higher than the materialist egalitarian principles of the State. Either this, or we are doomed to live as if through a movie running backwards as the horrendous debt required to create the socialist nightmare in the first place continues to destroy the nation.

But this has been a book on the Constitution. And so we must never forget one crucial point. It was the circumvention of our own Constitution, and the imposition of the Charter of Rights and Freedoms in 1982, that enabled the forcing of a vast bi-racial, bilingual, redistributionist/socialist program from the top down on an unsuspecting nation. In other words, the nation's current political impasse has resulted from a defilement of the essence of a constitution (that constitutions should be about rules, not deals).

In effect, the people's constitution was used against them. But then, this is the danger, and perhaps the inevitable end, of all written constitutions.

*   *   *

And so there is work to be done. For the solution to our troubles will not come from any written constitution, but from the unwritten constitution: from the minds and hearts of the people as they reconsider and then restore the founding values of their nation. This will require a new solidarity and belief in eternal, rock-solid principles: without these principles, euphoric paper constitutions have no meaning; with them, attempts to corrupt the constitution cannot possibly succeed. Such principles, deeply held and clearly articulated, are the only possible shield to protect the people against the ceaseless claims of interest groups, radical ideologues, politicians, and tax-mongers of all kinds. The living constitution, in other words, lies in the passion of the people for the basic values and principles by which they choose to live, not in any piece of paper. But where there are no values or principles, or where these are forgotten, or undefended, there can be no passion but only confusion and narrow self-interest. Such a people is soon easily corrupted.

So our first duty as a people is to reflect, to read, to comprehend. And then to stand and speak boldly against the enormous engines of big government and special interests, until they fall defeated. For this to happen, every man and woman must be able to say:

"I will not ask favours for my vote, and my vote cannot be bought. My freedom lies in me, not in the government, and I expect to exercise it by my own lights under a just law that is the same for all. Call me a citizen, and nothing else, for I want to be equal to all other citizens before the law, with no special rights or privileges over them, with no exceptions for me, or them, for my neighbour, my province, or those who govern me.

"I want to be left to my work, my family, my friends, my community, and my dreams of a nation in which we speak much less of rights and more of duties. I want to rise by my own efforts, and I only want help if I truly fail, and only then if friends and family fail me first. I want no one forcing any language upon me, my children, or my enterprise. I want to sell my labour and my goods to my fellow citizens unimpeded, and ask what I will, and receive what I can. And I will not be taxed in any way unless, with the people, I vote directly on how much. In this way, we will always know the difference between giving to the common good, at the least cost, and having what is ours taken by force to be squandered.

"I consent to be governed only by those who promise to serve the people, and if they end by serving themselves, I insist on the right to remove them. I want to speak my mind openly and freely within the bounds of truth and human decency. I insist on a government with the wisdom to know that the least government is best; that the State is a device invented by the people to serve their interests, not to serve its own interests, and that it serves the people best by restraining itself. And so I want the means to remove quickly from power those who would lead us into fiscal ruin. To protect citizens from oppression by those who think might is always right, I will fight for a community of sovereign provinces in a sovereign nation, with clearly divided powers, and always in principle resist the encroachment of a higher government upon any lower one. For my efforts and my property are my own, and I relish the duty to protect myself and my family for the future.

"Therefore I reject any notion of a constitutional right to things provided by others, because such false rights by nature defile the independence of both parties. Thus I accept all laws that wisely forbid me to behave in certain ways, but not laws that force me to behave in any way, whatsoever. And so all the laws to which I agree to submit must ultimately be made, altered, or ended by the people, and the people alone. Such a free society must grow naturally, under a just law, from the several wishes of the people, and I will not allow it to be bent by government program or policy to serve the visions of any man, or party, or judge, or written constitution.

"If I agree to live under any constitution it will be one that ensures my rights and freedoms against the government, not by the government. I insist on a government of laws, and not a government of men, and a constitution that by due effort and persuasion the people may change at will in order to remain free."

Notes

1. See Pierre Elliott Trudeau, *Federalism and the French Canadians* (Toronto: Macmillan, 1968). These quotations are from his chapter "The Practice and Theory of Federalism" (by the term *federalism*, he increasingly meant centralism). It is rather astonishing to see with what reluctance, even with what visceral resistance, supporters of Trudeau and his "liberal" policies acknowledge their hero's socialist beliefs. I have referred to him as a boutique intellectual because he skimmed like a honeybee over the surface of a variety of political subjects, stopping to sniff, to pick up a few sweet-sounding notions, then flitted on. Although his socialist ideas may well prove to be the ruin of Canada as a nation, he really only dabbled in socialist theory, even as he fancied himself a defender of freedom. His admirers ought to read his book carefully, whence they will take a proper fright.

2. Stephen Clarkson and Christina McCall, *Trudeau and Our Times* (Toronto: McClelland and Stewart, 1991), pp. 49, 121.

3. See his first book, *Federalism and the French Canadians*, and his last polemical book, *Pierre Trudeau Speaks Out on Meech Lake* (Toronto: General Paperbacks, 1990), in both of which Rousseau's phrase appears repeatedly. We may hope that some day a serious scholar will carefully analyse the fiery but flippant, and intellectually intriguing but self-contradictory, arguments and policies of this former prime minister of Canada.

4. *Trudeau and Our Times*, op. cit., p. 248.

5. Felix Morley, *Freedom and Federalism* (Indianapolis: Liberty Press, 1981), p. 33. This edition was reprinted from his first, 1959 edition.

6. Jean-Jacques Rousseau, *The Social Contract* (New York: Dutton, 1966), p. 15.

7. Trudeau, "Constituent Power, Sovereignty, and the Constitution," in A. R. Riggs and Tom Velk, eds., *Federalism in Peril* (Vancouver: the Fraser Institute, 1992).

8. Paul Johnson, "Is Totalitarianism Dead?" in *Crisis: A Journal of Lay Catholic Opinion*, February 1989.

9. Trudeau, in Riggs and Velk, *Federalism in Peril*, p. 28.

10. Benito Mussolini, "Fascism," in Goldwin, Lerner, Stourzh, eds., *Readings in World Politics* (Chicago: American Foundation for Political Education, 1951), vol. 1, pp. 66-70. This remarkably clear essay was translated from the *Enciclopedia Italiana*. It is a shame that Western intellectuals have so thoughtlessly accepted the Marxist view that fascism is a "right-wing" phenomenon. In fact, Communism and Fascism were rival brands of socialism — which is why Marxists worked so hard to condemn it. Marxists/Communists focused on an abstract international class struggle, on world socialism. It was not nation-based. Whereas Fascism focused on national, internal socialism. It powerfully co-opted nationalist feelings related to blood, culture, mythology, war, and the exercise of national political will. But both attacked the middle class and conservatives generally, were mass movements, violently atheistic, philosophically anti-liberal, socially deterministic, and economically collectivist. An excellent survey of the resurgent fascist phenomenon and its relation to "postmodern" efforts to restructure Western civilization,

mostly from within the universities of the West, is Gene Edward Veith Jr., *Modern Fascism: Liquidating the Judeo-Christian Worldview* (St. Louis: Concordia Publishing, 1993).

11. See the erratic, brilliant, and immensely suggestive polemic of Erik von Kuehnelt-Leddihn, *Leftism Revisited: From De Sade and Marx to Hitler and Pol Pot* (Washington: Regnery Gateway, 1990), especially his early chapters on the cultural and theological origins of European leftism, and the chapters on the rise of Marxism and Nazism.

12. Figures from Nielsen Marketing Research, Markham, Ontario.

13. Alexis de Tocqueville, *Democracy in America* (New York: Random House, 1990), vol. 2, p. 319.

14. A bracing and elegant essay on this topic is Bertrand de Jouvenel, *The Ethics of Redistribution* (Indianapolis: Liberty Press, 1990), first published in 1952.

15. I have borrowed a few thoughts and the terms "rulers' law" and "people's law" from an edifying little book by political scientists W. Cleon Skousen and Robert N. Thompson, entitled *Canada Can Now Adopt a Model Constitution* (Langley, British Columbia: Freeman Education Institute, 1982). Alas, few listened to them.

16. These points are drawn from Colin Rhys Lovell, *The English Constitution and Legal History* (New York: Oxford University Press, 1962), and as summarized in Skousen and Thompson, *Canada Can Now Adopt a Model Constitution*, note 2, p. 2.

17. Edmund Burke, *Reflections on the Revolution in France* (London: Penguin Books, 1968). This passionate and powerfully written treatise, in combination with *The Federalist Papers* (London: Penguin, 1987), the latter authored by three of the signers of the U.S.

Constitution, Madison, Hamilton, and Jay, together serve up enough solid political and moral principles to last a lifetime.

18. Thanks to my friend Kenneth McDonald for his emphasis on this contemptible deformation of the spirit of Canada's Constitution.

19. Much instruction can be gained on this whole matter, as in this distinction between constitutions deemed a consequence, as distinct from a source, of rights, from the great constitutional scholar A. V. Dicey, *Introduction to the Study of the Law of the Constitution* (Indianapolis: Liberty Classics, 1982).

20. The philosopher Jean-Paul Sartre turned away from his earlier philosophy of freedom as expressed in his *Being and Nothingness*, because he saw the restrictions of poverty, or class, as akin to a jail, and therefore concluded that human freedom was meaningless for most people. Then he turned to write a sour and almost unreadable treatise attempting to blend the determinism of Marx with the philosophy of freedom, in *Critique of Dialectical Reason*. The book was never finished, because it cannot be finished. The two explanations of human life cannot be reconciled, any more than we can reconcile place and motion in physics — the quandary of Zeno's arrow: by the time we say where the arrow is, it has moved somewhere else. By the same token, life obviously moves, evolves, changes, like the arrow, and any deterministic explanation of its outcome at any point in time is soon superseded by more ongoing change, and human change results in large measure from free choice.

21. A most instructive book on matters touching the nature of freedom, is Morley, *Freedom and Federalism* (Indianapolis, Liberty Press, 1981).

22. Ibid., p. 124.

23. The Charter contains a clause (section 26) which states that "the guarantee in this Charter of certain rights and freedoms shall not be construed as denying the existence of any other rights or freedoms that exist in Canada." Well now . . . let's see. The judge reads this and says, "I don't *deny their existence*, but I don't like 'em, either. Down with 'em!" What Canadians don't yet realize is that when questions arise as to the validity of these other, mostly common-law freedoms, they will automatically be subordinated to the Charter, which is now the "supreme law of Canada" — and any law conflicting with the Charter is "of no force or effect" (section 52).

24. In Morley, *Freedom and Federalism*, p. 306. I am grateful to Morley's fine discussions and distinctions with respect to federalism, democracy, and the process by which brute majority rule, if unchecked, smothers individual freedoms.

25. Dicey, op.cit., lxv.

26. Ibid., p. 121.

27. A stimulating essay on this general topic is Bertrand de Jouvenel, *The Ethics of Redistribution* (Indianapolis: Liberty Press, 1990; first published in 1950, by Cambridge University). The book is remarkable in that it dismisses all the arguments over the economic efficiency or counter-efficiency of redistribution, for the view that redistribution by its nature suppresses property, therefore freedom, and in democracies serves to oppress minorities and favour interest groups that manage to seize the levers of bureaucratic power.

28. John Robson, "The House That Tom Built," in *Fraser Forum* (Vancouver: the Fraser Institute, September 1993).

29. Several groups in Canada have proposed such a plan, such as the Tax Limit Coalition of British Columbia. See the editorial in *The Financial Post*, January 13, 1994.

30. The most compelling book on this dynamic of decline is Robert Nisbet's *The Quest for Community: A Study in the Ethics of Order and Freedom* (San Francisco: Institute for Contemporary Studies, 1990). This prescient book was first published in 1953, during the emergence from the debacle of World War Two, and provides a powerful overview of social decay since ancient times.

31. Morley, *Freedom and Federalism*, p. 39.

32. Quoted in *The Charter of Rights and Freedoms: A Guide for Canadians* (Ottawa: Ministry of Supply and Services, 1982), p. 29.

33. From a complete verbatim copy of his speech.

34. This segment is from a transcript of a revealing discussion with Trudeau, and published as "Constitutent Power, Sovereignty, and the Constitution," in A. R. Riggs and Tom Velk, eds., *Federalism in Peril* (Vancouver: the Fraser Institute, 1992).

35. William Johnson, "Separatism and the Quebec Intellectual Tradition," in Riggs and Velk, *Federalism in Peril*, p. 145.

36. J. L. Granatstein and David Stafford, "Shadow Play," *Saturday Night*, October 1990.

37. Stephen A. Scott, "Secession or Reform," *Federalism in Peril*, p. 157.

38. Kenneth McNaught, "A Ghost at the Banquet: Could Quebec Secede Peacefully?" in J. L. Granatstein and Kenneth McNaught, *"English Canada" Speaks Out* (Toronto: Doubleday, 1991), p. 90.

39. See ibid., p. 80, for a good survey of this violence.

40. A good brief summary of the half-dozen published arguments for partition put forth by Canadians can be found in Scott Reid, *Canada Remapped* (Vancouver: Pulp Press, 1992). The summary includes those

by Jacques Brossard, *L'accession à la souveraineté et le cas du Québec* (1976); Lionel Albert and William Shaw, *Partition: The Price of Quebec's Independence* (1980), a detailed, historical and treaty-based work; Kenneth McDonald, *Keeping Canada Together* (1990), which spells out in no uncertain terms what partition could mean. This book traces the effect of Quebec's influence, and advocates returning power to the majority through referendums, balanced budgets, and a renewed federalism, with Ottawa confined to national matters — seven departments instead of twenty-six. The summary also includes David Bercuson and Barry Cooper, *Deconfederation: Canada Without Quebec* (1991), a book by two western professors who suggest that because there are no legal mechanisms for separation or partition, Canada should dictate terms of partition to Quebec, and would be better off without Quebec; Ian Ross Robertson, whose tough proposals for a neutral corridor can be found in Granatstein and McNaught, *"English Canada" Speaks Out* (1991); David Varty, *Who Gets Ungava* (1991), an examination of the legal grounds. Scott's book is itself a level-headed plea to establish the legal framework for partition now, before the fur flies, and to use a Swiss-style referendum and enclave format.

41. J. L. Granatstein, "Canada, Quebec and the World," in J. L. Granatstein and Kenneth McNaught, eds., *"English Canada" Speaks Out*, p. 105.